CW01500082

Trying to Fool Death

ALSO BY MARVIN COHEN

The Self-Devoted Friend, Rapp and Carroll, 1967; New Directions, 1967; Tough Poets Press, 2nd (with introduction), 2017

Dialogues, Turret Books, 1967

The Monday Rhetoric of the Love Club and Other Parables, Rapp and Whiting, 1973; New Directions, 1973

Baseball the Beautiful: Decoding the Diamond, Links Books, 1974; Tough Poets Press, 2nd (expanded) as: *Baseball as Metaphysics*, 2017

Fables at Life's Expense, Latitudes Press, 1975

Others, Including Morstive Sternbump, Bobbs-Merrill, 1976; Tough Poets Press, 2nd (with interview), 2016

The Inconvenience of Living and Other Acts of Folly, Urizen Books, 1977

How the Snake Emerged from the Bamboo Pole but Man Emerged from Both, Oasis Books/Earthgrip Press, 1978

Aesthetics in Life and Art, Existence in Function and Essence and Whatever Else is Important Too, Gull Books, 1982

How to Outthink a Wall: An Anthology, Verbivoracious Press, 2016 (includes all previous anthologies and some new pieces)

Five Fictions, Tough Poets Press, 2018

Inside the World: As Al Lehman, Sagging Meniscus Press, 2018

Women, and Tom Gervasi, Sagging Meniscus Press, 2018

Run Out of Prose, Sagging Meniscus Press, 2018

Sadness Corrected, Sagging Meniscus Press, 2019

Life's Tumultuous Party: Reduced to its Essential Partycycles, Sagging Meniscus Press, 2020

Plays on Words, Tough Poets Press, 2020

Conversations and Versifications, Tough Poets Press, 2021

Questions To Be Asked Before Proceeding, Tough Poets Press, 2021

The Hard Life of a Stone and Other Thoughts, Sagging Meniscus Press, 2021

BooBoo Roi: A Murdered Murderer Too Soon, Sagging Meniscus Press, 2021

Necessary Ends, Broadway Play Publishing Inc, 2022 (reprinted from *Plays from the New York Shakespeare Festival*)

Marvin Cohen

Trying to Fool Death

or

One Thing After Another

Edited by Colin Myers

Tough Poets Press
Arlington, Massachusetts

Copyright © 2023 by Marvin Cohen

Preface copyright © 2023 by Colin Myers

ISBN 979-8-218-19101-6

Tough Poets Press
Arlington, Massachusetts 02476
U.S.A.

www.toughpoets.com

I dedicate this book to Maggie Beale;
a voice so illustratively real.
— *Marvin Cohen*

And many thanks to Maggie Beale
for her help in editing this book
and her general loveliness.
— *Colin Myers*

PREFACE

This book comprises verse and dialogues drawn from Marvin's almost daily emails to a group of friends. It focuses on Marvin's acute awareness of his mortality; on death and living, on memories, on friendship and lost friends. The pieces obsessively work and rework these themes, with a viewpoint varying from the joyous to the despairing, and from the stark to the absurd.

To help achieve his goals, Marvin delights in tropes such as conundrums, contradiction, punning, extended lists and elegant variation. He revels in long, complex titles for both dialogue and poetry, sometimes to the extent that his titles can be read as separate pieces. In his poems he likes multiple rhymes and dubious half-rhymes whilst foregoing formal rhythms, but in his dialogues he is happy to burst into verse.

Here are two typical critical observations:

"In Marvin Cohen one senses the metaphysical thirst, as he questions the notion of reality, as he distorts accepted relationships of time and death, as he approaches dark subjects with the good-natured humour reminiscent of Benjamin Péret, and particularly as he demonstrates his extraordinary power over words and words associations that break down the expected ones."[1]

"Marvin Cohen's texts are monologues of a mind trying to fix itself and experience in speech, to give voice to experience and time which it realizes cannot be mastered by its available tools— consciousness and language. The voice which animates these self-conscious and amused texts delights in its fictiveness, making itself a self-conscious artifice in which the mind's persona achieves a degree of abstraction that makes it read like an essay."[2]

Not surprisingly, Marvin Cohen's work is not only compared to such the authors as Donald Barthelme, Samuel Beckett and James Thurber; but also to the graphic work of Saul Steinberg; the films of Buster Keaton and the Marx Brothers; and to the Surrealists in general.

Marvin Cohen, himself, says:

"I like odd things that are semi-realistic and that have a kind of curveball catch to it," Cohen says, explaining his style. "So that it's ambiguous, ambivalent; you can read a few things in a sentence at the same time. It's not just a journalistic, flat literal sentence, not like 'The girl went to the tree and picked a pear.' Some kind of irony should be welded into it."[3]

"When I use words, one word leads to another and then my mind kind of works along puns and double entendre, whereby there is ambiguity in a phrase. In poetry, a lot of phrases could be interpreted in a few different ways. You need further embellishment for the next word or the next phrases. I don't think along journalistic lines when I write. When I write, I write and put in jazz. . . . When I start out on a piece of writing, I may have a vague concept that amuses me and is pregnant with possibilities. I'd like to give it body. To attempt a train of words. Where one word, or one sentence, or the beginning phrase can set the stage for what may follow. I have to make the second sentence come in harmony with the first sentence, but they have a counterpoint. . . . So, the sequence of words goes on and is playful. I see the sequence of writing as playful, where one sentence follows and compliments another sentence, and then you can't stop there because now you are in a groove. Then a third sentence comes on and you are having fun and now you are in business. Now a fourth sentence comes and now you have momentum because you've built up a sequence. It's like how nature builds up DNA."[4]

The pieces here are printed in the order that they arrived by email and as such they serve as a diary of Marvin's thoughts. However, this book can be read in any sequence; it's a book to dip into and then dip into again, to read out loud to yourself and to others to catch its cadences and subtleties.

Colin Myers

1. Anna Balakian, *Surrealism: The Road to the Absolute*, 1984.
2. Charles Russell, Avant-Garde Today. 1981.
3. Ross Barkan, "Surreal Surreal Genius: Why Onetime Literary Hotshot Marvin Cohen Deserves Another Look," *Village Voice*, 11/23/2016.
4. Nina Buckless: "The Drumbeat of Society," FictionWritersReview.com, 6/12/2017.

BY WAY OF AN AUTHOR'S INTRODUCTION

[*The following is a transcript of a 2018 video taken in the park outside Marvin's East Village apartment block.*†]

> Too late, now, to have any more sex.
> That period in my life is now an ex.
> The culprit, of course, is old age,
> causing me, in life's book, to turn the page.
> I'm impotent, but I'm also a sage.
> My old cock is docile in its cage.
> So pity me, you young folks.
> I no longer produce those powerful pokes.
> They're reduced to a series of jokes.
> ["The Permanent Interruption," 2018]

Boy, what a poem! *(Chortles.)*

Well everybody talks about the current time in his life. So that the current time in my life is eking out into death. I'm pre-death, so in my nervousness and apprehension, I've got to bolster my courage so writing things down and spelling them out may somehow reconcile me with my horrible faith ahead. Faith no! Fate yes, right.

> I'm living myself out of life,
> soon I'll run out of time
> and in turn time romps away from me
> at an equestrian pace
> time is the darkest doom
> that neatly prepares nobody's tomb.

Well, all of this I know, it's very death-pronounced and lopsided and I guess it's the product of this miserable period of having fun while old age has incapacitated me from having fun. If you look at

9

it from a certain viewpoint, we need to make room for new people. So evolution clears old people away so that new people can come along with their new gadgets and new improvisations of mechanical instruments.

(Shows recent Tough Poet Press editions of his books.) And now I've recently started a renaissance of being rediscovered. There are reprints of publications in the 1970s. Some were plays, some were novels, some were essays, some were humor pieces, some were poems. So it varies, I have no real tag after my name. I'm kind of lost in the scattering and smattering of little books that have not realized fame even for fifteen minutes. But that's okay, because I'm happily married and I'm reconciled to impending death. *(Smiles.)* I'm married, happily, to sweet Candace. She is religious but I manage to be happy anyway— you can put up with something. She doesn't foist her religion on me, though in the language of Brooklyn: it comes 'foyst' for her.

Eternity, infinity: those are big words, and often they convey meaninglessness.

> Death is supreme. To defy it, religion
> tries to weave its holy magic,
> but death is firm in its reality
> and poor religion is left gasping at the gate
> ["How 'Nothing' Stands in the Way," 2018]

Boy, is that pessimistic! I guess I must have had spiritual impulses because I felt somehow 'One with everything.' Just like sometimes I approach a hot-dog vendor, and he says "How would you like it?" and I say "Make me one with everything." And I relished saying that! I catch up on my joke!

Okay, I grew up in Brooklyn, not far from Coney Island. Well, for me it was a little different because from the age of three I got hard of hearing with diseases in my ear; we were poor and my mother and father seemed like strangers and I didn't get much guidance. And I wasn't in the same wavelength or drumbeat as other people because they followed what they heard and I didn't hear it. I was kind of an oddball. I was lonely, yes, because I felt somehow that I was uncompoundable and I felt that maybe I'm too odd to marry. And one way I managed to not be isolated from other people was humor and comedy—seeing things at odd angles, analogies and metaphors, and that other people would be interested in that. I won them over by making jokes and that way they would acknowledge me as somebody to be entertained by.

> I grew up, but lived so full a life
> by the mechanical count of mere years,
> that now, longevity's survivor,
> my body falls into a preparation for death,
> and not my own fault, but I have to go.
> My brain has cooled down, and I'm drugged.
> My verbalized thinking enters a feeble stage
> and having known many people, I drift away
> escorted by the blunt hand of pain.
>   ["An Undetailed Account of Life," 2018]

Sorry, sorry. But I was ultra romantic and I tended too fall in love too easily whereas the women acted as if I was too needy. If I had only been more aloof then I would have gotten more women. That was the age of sexual revolution—actually I would call it an evolution.

(Distracted by squirrel.) Oh look, there's a squirrel with a nut! Ever since I've gotten older, older and older—so now I'm such an old man that younger people look through me and pass me as if I don't exist. Because they don't want to be reminded what's in store for them so they better leave me alone. Live it up, have fun and snarl with some sarcasm and be sadistic—no, not sadistic: sarcastic. Somehow live it

and lump it. If you're going to be old you might as well be old. If you get impotent and there's no chance for you with a lady that you may encounter then be sad and have nostalgia for the good old days when you were able to get a girl.

> Humans, that's what we are,
> no other way we could have been born
> Give me examples, for instance.
> Well, the generalities pile up
> and the specifics are too numerous.
> People tell their stories
> and look for the listeners.
> The listeners and the tellers
> are what we principally are.
> ["Aspects of Our Kind," 2018]

So I do what I can; and life is a sweetheart you still embrace it for all that's left of you and that's left of us.

[† *"Meet Marvin Cohen," 2018 (youtu.be/ckbFD2Ufvmw). See also: "At the Cornelia Street Cafe," 2018, (youtu.be/dShk0nHqDgo) and other short videos by Williams Cole on YouTube. Williams Cole has been producing, directing and editing documentary features and short profiles for over 20 years. His father, the book editor and wit Bill Cole, was best man at Marvin's wedding.*]

REFLECTIONS AT NINETY
VERSED EVER SO NICELY

Getting to ninety is a risky age.
Are you turning near the last page?
Memories carpet and rug your past.
What's forward in front? Don't ask.
Eke out the rest of your life
ill protected from mountains of strife
with your body quite almost breaking down
with senile loss of functions.
You'll enjoy no more carefree luncheons
with all your old pals.
They're all entirely dead—the boys and gals.
The world was a great place to live in.
But now the time has come to give in.
Was I grateful? Every day.
Work got tedious, but never the play.
Thus memory will assert
till cozily swept over by dirt
just in time. I can't bear the hurt.

THE DECISIVE MAN AND HIS EQUAL COMPANION

The more you value life with great appreciation, the more you fear death?

Sure. Death is the arch depriver.

But doesn't old age, which precedes death, do already most of death's later job?

Sure. But old age is still more fun than death. That's where the memories come out in full array.

But isn't nostalgia mostly painful?

I'll take it over death any day.

Well, you're a decisive character.

Once my mind is made up, it either stays that way or I change it.

You sure own a lot of versatility.

Yeah, it sprawls over. I gotta put it in order some day.

Does writing help you?

Yeah, it puts one word after another.

But life often goes backwards.

Reversal straightens it out.

Is life sometimes a mix-match?

That's it, no matter how large the batch.

Something good from this has got to hatch.

You curl up your glove and make the catch.

DIALOGUE OF FUTILE ENDEAVOR

Is life so vast that it's beyond definition?

Yes. Definition is too small and neat to encompass life's enormous, unruly scale.

Nevertheless, can you put the whole extent of life into a tiny nutshell for its essential brief definition?

No. The details overwhelm me in their endless miscellany that resists convenient categorizations.

"Essence" is a way of shortening the procedure.

Let's bypass "definition," and proceed to "essence" in our attempt to shorten our manufactured brevity? It won't work.

So just plainly let me put it: "What is life?"

Don't trick me. Life is too slippery elusive to fit any narrow puny defining. It runs away.

Run after it.

You do so. Good luck. I stay put.

Where is "put"?

Right in the middle. Where everything is evident.

LIFE VERSUS NOTHINGNESS

Birth is a lucky break occasioned by your parents' sex connection, whether they're married or not. Once you're launched as a baby, it's instinctive that even as an orphan, charitable institutions manage to take care of you. Or somehow you're on your way to being reared by legal parents, or whoever. You get to youth, maturity, middle age, old age, and eventually death; never to heaven: the whole deal except mythology. But you only get what's possible. But in most cases, that's more than plenty. But once it's over, that's *it*, and it's like the whole process never happened.

Is the nothingness after death identical to the nothingness before your embryo?

In effect, yes.

That sounds pretty cold.

Only the way it's read. There's no "cold" in nothingness, which excludes such human elements, like values.

Give me warmth and light, but not too much of either.

Spoken like a true product of evolution's most intellectual species.

THE "OPPOSITES" DIALOGUE

Life and death, being opposites, are radically unlike a man and a woman, being opposites.

How so?

A person's life and death can never co-exist. But a man and a woman can very much co-exist, and often do.

How clever of you to figure that out! What about day and night being opposites?

They each operate within a twenty-four hour time framework, and take turns alternately.

Again, how clever! What about east and west being opposites? And also north and south?

Those are geographical oppositions, requiring space extensions on all ends.

I can barely wrap my mind around those concepts without imaginary visualizing. What about war and peace being opposites?

That's a sequence, wherein peace is followed by war, and war by peace.

Those are historical concepts, involving time's passages.

How right you are! What about heavy and light as weight concepts?

Indeed! I agree with you.

I'm glad you're so agreeable.

That leads me to "like" and "dislike" being opposites.

That's a matter of tastes, feelings, and preferences.

How about youth and age? Are they opposites?

That's a lifetime matter, expanding from birth to death.

That's going too far. When I hear "death," it has a foul ring,

being immortally an ugly thing.
I treat it with revulsion,
but can never hope for its expulsion.

BRING HONESTY AND TRUTH BACK.
DON'T BE A TRAITOROUS HACK
WHOSE INTEGRITY HAS NOTABLE LACK.

Life is full of contradictions.
Realities appear like fictions.
What am I in the world to believe?
Has truth disappeared? I grieve.
What can I pin down to real facts?
but can never hope for its expulsion.
Is perception full of voluntary acts?
Have imagination and I connived pacts?
Just what is the meaning of life
aside from the inevitability of strife?
Is the world imagination's figment?
Is horsehide confused with pigment?
If you connect the dots everywhere,
will they converge? Or dissolve in the air?
Perception gives me a false conception
of architecture continually corrected.
To make fantasy the world's ruler
is to stifle truth all the crueler.
Tamper with honesty, and you're a fooler.
Make integrity the biggest factor
and you its accredited actor.

IS HEAVEN LITERALLY REAL
BEYOND IMAGINATION'S LYRICAL FEEL?

Heaven simply doesn't exist,
though the stubborn religionist
will repeatedly persist.
Heaven isn't on reality's list.
It's outside the world's contours,
though travel companies conduct tours
to include heaven's allures.
Heaven is an obvious myth
with no known length or width.
You have to do without, not with.
It lacks dimensionality,
which is a heightened fallacy.
Thus when you die, don't expect
a hint or glimpse, in any respect,
of heaven on your dead intellect.
Other considerations are wrecked,
so far as science must detect.
Heaven is no more real
than a buried corpse can truly feel,
as the world turns on its own wheel.
On this, I rest my appeal.
If the court will approve,
I don't need to further prove.
Common sense is my witness
to prove my argument's fitness.
Sentimentality is less
with no god to bless.
Thus I atheistically confess.

EXTRAORDINARY FRIENDSHIP

Jimmy Stagno is gone forever.
He was my pal, but we had to sever.
We knew each other over seventy years,
sharing all our joys and fears
in growing up together
in every single possible weather.
His death put an abrupt end
to our being each other's friend,
which not even memory can mend,
which remains in my stubborn skull.
Without Jimmy, life is somehow dull.
We had so many a laugh together
and commiseration no matter whether.
We played ball in deed and mind,
and naturally we were always kind.
Our friendship was a tribute to love.
He moves gently, just barely above.
His image I frequently catch
to consummate our unique match.
I see him briefly now and then,
celebrating the past's constant "when."
There he is, soaring again.
His memory produces tears
to wash away the years.
I'm left to face the lonely fears.
Suddenly his face re-appears.

DOUBT DEBATES DETERMINATION

My fear of death becomes more and more realistic, the older I get.

That's understandable. Nothing you can do about it.

Yes, I can do something: Go to heaven directly after death.

Aren't you resorting to myth?—which in realistic terms is a lie?

Lie or not, I'll get to heaven by any means necessary.

You're stupidly determined.

The end justifies the means.

What means will you use?

Theology and prayer. Christ is my guy. Through Him I'll conquer death.

Good luck on that futile enterprise.

Your doubt sticks out all over you. Our friendship is over.

It'll return when your delusion is over.

I'll mock you from Heaven, you limited earthling!

You were always stupid, from your very birthling.

GIVE LIFE A SLIGHT COMEBACK
ON DEATH'S OTHERWISE IMMOVABLE TRACK.

Life is an eternal mystery.
Metaphysics attempts its history,
but fails to persuade.
Philosophy is of no aid.
Once lived, life is torn away
and never sees another day.
Death nullifies everything around,
and ears are blasted of their sound.

Couldn't life have been spread out
so that something of it is left to sprout
along death's desolate area
to make the afterlife seem more airy,
and the denuded skin be more hairy?
Why does death have to be a solid block
whose confines are under key and lock?
Give life a fleeting glimpse
free of death's annoying imps.
Give death some nostalgia,
despite including life's neuralgia.
Let life occasionally revive
in death's guts and come alive.
Is my request too bold,
so that reality now has to scold?

ACCEPTING LIFE, NO MATTER WHAT.

In life, you can't always get that you want.
In death, you're spared that frustration.
That doesn't make death a wonderful example to follow.
Keep life, though it's sometimes hard to swallow.
Death is deplorably shallow.
In life, there's much to allow.

PAST AND PRESENT
ARE STILL EFFERVESCENT.

When I was in my sexual prime,
many a woman I would climb.
Now that old age has beset me,
sexual conquest can't get me

the high pride I was used to.
Loneliness has me all bruised through
where once love and romance grew.
Of my women-filled life, no one is new.
So what's ahead? Maybe to die
after looking back and having a good cry,
and braving nostalgia with a deep sigh.
In my grave I'm going to lie
and forget how wonderful I was as a guy.
Do I leave behind a live woman to cry?
I'll be too dead to ever know the effect of the love I had to bestow,
looking up from too far below.

THE DEATH DIALOGUE
WHICH IS NEVER A PROLOGUE.
THERE'S NO "AFTER"
FROM BASEMENT TO RAFTER.
IT'S NO OCCASION FOR LAUGHTER.

Old age weakens me into a passive state.

Then are you a pushover for Death's aggression?

I fall willingly into his possession.

Then does your brain stop being conscious?

It drops out of my skull and has no pulse.

You can't even experience something else?

No. I take an eternal "rest."

Does oblivion stop your perception?

The world is lost to my senses.

You're in no world, but float away?

Done are activities like work and play.

Is it ever possible to revive?

No. I'm done with being alive.

Is it all over for you in identity?

Death guards me with empty preventity.

IDENTIFYING

Aren't you tired sometimes of being only yourself and no one else?

Sure, but I'm stuck with it.

Do you sometimes pretend you're someone else?

Yes, I often identify with characters from a novel or a movie or a play.

And that takes you out from yourself?

Temporarily only.

Then you return to being you?

Yes, who else? There are no other candidates.

Are you bored by yourself?

Not when I'm having fun.

Yes, having fun is a great feeling.

Sure. We all sometimes have that feeling.

That unites us as humans.

Having pain and misery also does.

Well, that's life for you.

Not only for me. For everyone else.

"Everyone else" is a lot of people to identify yourself with.

I'm in it with them. My pals.

Is the human race that united?

No. We pals disagree often.

Well, forgive them. It's the nature of the beast.

Are you calling my pals beasts? Then I include myself.

There'd be no politics without disagreement.

Or just disputes between two people. Even by man and wife.

Discord is on every level.

I blame it on the devil.

But there *is* no "devil." There's only us.

Thanks for locating the fuss.

THE "SPAN" DIALOGUE

From birth to death is one span?

From sperm-egg embryo to "the last gasp" is one span.

After "the last gasp," that mortal border ends?

Well, the mortal border begins the separation taking effect.

Well, it was good while it lasted.

Not necessarily only "good." Some philosophers define life as "hell."

Sometimes. I'd say life is a "mixed bag."

That's a safe definition. It sure can be a miscellaneous motley. Or in musical terms, "medley."

You sure are safe in saying that.

Thanks. Being a mathematician, I like precision.

How far along in life are you?

I'd say approximately . . .

You don't have to answer my question, which may be too personal.

I don't have enough vanity to consider it personal. I'm not touchy.

I like an open spirit like you.

IN CHILDHOOD I COULD TOUCH.
BUT NOW MEMORIES DO AS SUCH.

In childhood I played with material objects
like leaden toy soldiers
and aluminum toy cars
and even rubber guns.
Now that my age is old,
what I play with are mental images,
called memories, of all my years
since childhood's joys and tears:
years so full and abundant,
with so many of them,
old age weeps a tear or two
with so much to go through
of so many recollections
more abundant than old stamp collections.
I swallow too many, like caramel confections,
to ruin my teeth with dental infections.
How intimate are the connections!
I'm addicted to remember too much,
which I can only think of, but not touch.
They're golden reminiscences, as such.

BEING SOMEONE ELSE,
INSTEAD OF BEING LEFT ON A SHELF
WITH YOUR FED-UP USUAL SELF

It's always you, every day,
living the same old life
under the same identity,
starting with your given name.
Wouldn't you like to change places
and be someone else for a change?
Especially someone glamorous
like a heart-throb movie star
whom women flock to?
Or a Presidential power machine
who can phone the Russian dictator
in the middle of the very night
if your twin countries conduct a blight
that may lead to a global fight?
You'd be in charge of a universal fright
with your finger on the atomic bomb
to sound a historical alarm.
No thanks. Just go back to being you.
Daily and usual, you have enough to do,
enough minor management to get through.
But I do tire of my own life. Don't you?

ROBERT BURNS CELEBRATING NEW YEAR'S EVE.
SO MANY DEAR FRIENDS FOR WHOM TO GRIEVE
WITHOUT SO MUCH AS A "BY-YOUR-LEAVE!"

Old friends who are forgotten and never brought to mind
are too dead to even mind.
I think of them regularly,

both collectively and severally.
I have so many old dead friends,
that fallings-out don't have amends.
They dropped me or I dropped them,
without even a bare notion of "ahem."
My brain is a jumble of all of them,
so periodically I review them.
Memory is a tricky thing.
Which old friend should I now bring
to mind, as if hauling him up
brings back appetite when we used to sup?
My besotted mind is now going corrupt.
"Pardon me if I interrupt
your reveries," I tell myself.
"I'll pile them up and file them away
on my archival shelf."
Old friends in my rotting memory
were so friendly! But "enemies"
describe them at the end
too frequently. I'll make amends
to keep my mind from going round the bend
and losing a whole stockpile of dear friends.
May they forgive me for losing them wholesale
to forgetfulness'es giveaway sale.
It's like a market bazaar
that's gone crazy and bizarre.
Have I deteriorated that far?

THE OLD AGE DIALOGUE

I'm old and tired and internally sick. By looking at me, how long do
you give me before death calls it a day?

In your case, three or four more years, at the most.

How do you think I should fill them out?

With whatever old age pleasures and consolations you have left.

Any specifics?

Fill them out for yourself, given your own circumstances and preferences.

Any advice?

Take care of yourself.

I know that already.

Well, why come to me?

You look even older than me, so you've had experience.

Experience isn't everything.

But doesn't it add up?

Yes, but to what end?

Oh, shut up! As a conversationalist, you're the living end.

THE TIME DIALOGUE

I'm worried that old age might kill me.

Given a little more time, it will.

Is time the only thing that stands between me and my own death?

Time is the only thing you have to worry about.

Then how can I slow it up?

You can't. Time is gone before you know it.

Then time is my curse, my enemy.

At least you have a little left. Nurse it and cherish it.

But all ultimately in vain.

Well, you're helpless. Give up.

But not before my time.

Hoard it. Be a miser.

You're my true adviser.

THE "AVOIDING DEATH" DIALOGUE

I'm afraid of dying.

Big deal. So is everyone else. That doesn't make you a coward.

Thanks for the compliment.

Feeling brave is no virtue. Just be careful. Don't tempt death. Take no chances.

Are you advocating "Safety first"?

Sure. Keep alive as long as you can, by avoiding accidents. Not taking risks.

I won't be care-free, like a dare-devil. I'll preserve life with a close defensive game, allowing my old age to ripen into a delicious temptation for death. I'll be irresistible. I'll be death's heaven.

You're going too far. The aim is to *avoid* death, not to present yourself as an irresistible target.

I forgot my priorities. I was carried away.

Not by death, I hope.

THE "NOW," VERSUS THE "THEN," PROVES INFERIOR TO THAT OLD "WHEN."

The older I get, the closer to death,
so I mustn't over-do aging.
I should only be getting moderately old
but not excessively, all told.
The days of my prime
are far behind,
too much dangerously so.
I'm much too advanced in age
to counter death's opportunistic rage,
which willingly wipes me off the stage.
I've worked so hard: is this my wage?
No, I'm past needing money.
I used to spend it on my sweet honey
when we went to a fair on a Sunday.
Can we return to it ever some day?
No, death is too obstinate
to renew the good old times
in the merry ringing of time's chimes.

THE SLEEPY DIALOGUE

Last night when I went to bed, my sleepiness chanced upon an adversary: Insomnia.

Who won?

Insomnia's surprise attack earned him the victory, so Sleepiness was routed and had to wait a few hours.

Couldn't Insomnia have shown compassion and mercy, and given Sleepiness a break?

No chance. Insomnia is a vicious, aggressive battler, and refused compassion and mercy for its defeated combatant.

Poor Sleepiness. Did it ever have a chance later to catch up?

No. It had an early morning appointment at the office, so was red-eyed with fatigue at the job, so almost got me fired by the angry Boss; or if not fired, then a pay reduction.

Poor you. You were Insomnia's primary victim and incurred your Sleepiness'es wrath.

They're both my servants, but by fighting each other they used me as the primary victim in the first place. Imagine my fatigue!

You poor fellow! You should have them both fired!

No. When they work it out between them, they serve me well, and my main point being that they come cheap.

I don't know whether to congratulate you or pity you.

Compromise and give me both. I need all I can get.

Why? Is today's market terrible?

The worst. It dropped below the historical old Inflation.

I hope you're not inflating those statistics.

No. If anything, I'm minimizing them.

Good. Understatedness can be an endearing asset.

LOVE REMEMBERED IS NOT ONLY SEPTEMBERED, BUT ELEVEN MORE MONTHS TEMPERED.

Life is later a bundle of tears
that mope and grope on those early years.
My love and I went to the fair
when our mutual primes were ripe.
I spent money on her there,

now totally unregretted.
Then we went and settled down.
Now she's dead and I'm alive.
Like a quicksilver, she slipped through life
and left me all alone.
In her deepest memory, I groan.
Linked to her, there's no telephone.
Dearest love, I remember you now,
with old-age wrinkles mottling my brow.
I apologize for past offenses.
Now we're separated by a bunch of fences
with pointed spikes at the tops.
I apologize that the years are past,
since life and love were not made to last.
There's no end to my loving you
while my brains remain together,
unlike us. We're far apart.
But what are you doing in my constant heart?
I hope you're not inflating those statistics.

THE DOTTY DIALOGUE

Is life one damn thing after another?

Sure. If you go back long or far enough in retrospect, it's one damn thing *before* another.

Is there enough time for all that?

There has to be. Time is what prevents everything from occurring simultaneously.

Good. Each event in its proper *place*, which is a metaphor for *time*. Now I feel calmer, with my sense of order.

Order prevents mass insanity.

That's the excuse that dictators make in order to justify ordering people about.

Dictators forcibly inject order.

That's mass-political. But in individual life, we need order to think straight.

But some thoughts are more rewarding if they're *crooked*.

Is that where Absurdity and Surrealism come from?

Sure. They had to come from *some* where, to create delirious disorder.

Is "delirious disorder" just "creative originality"?

How poetic of you to make such a connection!

All I'm doing is connecting dots.

You're too dotty for me.

I could make the duplicate complaint.

THE TIME AND SPONTANEOUS FRIENDSHIP DIALOGUE

Sometimes I'm so sad; at other times I'm so happy. How can I sort Life out, in order to make sense of its unsettling contradictions?

Time itself sorts out Life's inconsistencies. Enough time is laid out for *one* thing to happen; then enough time is left empty for something totally *contradictory* to take place. Time is so large and vast in our lives, it can accommodate very disparate opposites to follow each other in various different directionary sequences.

If it weren't for time, everything would have to happen at once?

Yes, it would all come together, like an atom bomb extinguishing differences in one fell blast.

But that's too destructive.

Sorry. Anyway, enough time allows things and events to take place semi-orderly.

But then, what gets condensed?

Enough contradictions and simultaneities and coincidences occur, to call them mystical miracles or to pronounce simply the cliché that it's indeed "a small world."

That's how just now I met you and you met me. But friends are defined as those who make appointments. So let's be volitionary as friends, so as to not rely on rare accidents or coincidence to meet again, but through friendly deliberation and volition.

On that note, here's my phone number and Email address. Don't lose them.

In exchange, here's mine. See you soon.

"ANNOYING NERVOUSNESS" DIALOGUE

We know about the world to some extent, but what actually is life itself? Both our own human species, and all other forms of it?

How do I know? I'm not a scientist.

You don't have to be snappy. I was only asking a question. You act like I was rude or abrupt.

I wasn't prepared. Your curiosity seemed so impulsive, as if our lives depended on an immediate answer. What's your problem?

I've been feeling nervous lately.

Well, that's appropriate. The world is acting nerve-wracking, so you're reacting in keeping.

Thanks. Now I feel normal. If the world is going to act up, I'll respond in kind.

You're complimenting me, like I was a therapist.

You were forced into that role by circumstances.

Good. Now that you're cured, leave the world in peace.

You mean I should die?

Don't go *that* far.

THE "SHORT VERSION" DIALOGUE

Life is the going from one thing to another till finally you get too weak to live any more.

While you're going from one thing to another, you remember things of before. But remembering doesn't stop you from going on.

What does all this add up to?

That's it. That's the whole deal.

I thought there was more to life.

I've only dealt with its rudimentary stuff. I didn't add its glamour, romance, ornamentation—the fancy stuff.

They have to be factored in.

They are, daily and nightly.

Then everyone is a philosopher?

But they don't know it enough to take credit.

But some know it so well that they grab too much credit.

Why do you write?

To make collections of my connections that fit together.

Yeah, there's lots to go on.

It's what you make of it. That's life.

What's "god"?

There is none. There's just us. Inside the world.

What's the world?

Where we live. Till life ends.

Is that it?

The short version.

Some day, we'll go deeper.

That day may never come.

Well, that's life.

THE POSTERITY DIALOGUE

I'm about to die from old age. I had wanted fame as an author, but failed to get it at the deadline.

Posterity might give you one of its crowns.

Too late for me. I'm unable to cash in on my own posterity.

Your belated posterity triumphs may make your living survivors envious and jealous and resentful, not congratulatory toward you.

I predict their attitude toward me will be mere impersonal indifference.

Your survivors are egotists!

So would I be, if I joined them.

THE POSTHUMOUS FAME DIALOGUE

Posthumous success is impossible to enjoy.

So then if my books get famous, I won't be there to benefit.

All that time and effort you labored over them come to roost, but oblivious to you in death's empty state.

I would have cherished the egotistical benefit, but posthumously too late.

If you had been famous within life, you could have had an extra late-season romance with an enthusiastic woman admirer.

Yes, if still young enough to avoid impotence.

Time imposes so many factors!

My books and I lead separate lives, when time intervenes. Damn that intervention if my books turned out more successful than me, their author who died in the personal trappings of modesty, poverty, and literary failure.

THE "BANISHED FROM SOCIETY" DIALOGUE

Life pulsates with energy till it breaks down. Becoming dead automatically disqualifies you as a member of Society. They want only live-wires, to contribute to organic Society, those clean-cut smugs.

Being so old as to be on Death's verge, I notice snobbish members of Society giving me dirty looks, signifying I soon won't belong with them.

It's bad enough to have to die. But by that, to incur Society's contempt simply just adds to Death's intolerable impoverishment.

Society's attitude to me is: "You're not one of us. We don't want you if you have to die."

Well, I would exclude you too, if I were one of them.

But you're not. Being old enough, you're like me.

Just because you won't play ball with them, they don't want you in their private game, whose exclusivity entitles them to cruelly demean you.

Well, if they reject me, I reject them.

Death leaves you with no alternative. How can you fight back, in your bitter resentment?

At heart, I'm jealous of them.

Throw envy into the deal; I agree. Let's boycott Society.

But not with vulgar banners and picketing.

No, with heads high and proud,
and baying our protests aloud.

RESULTS FROM LIFE'S BATTLES
INCLUDE A THROAT THAT WEAKLY RATTLES.
EXTREME MELANCHOLY
RIDICULES LIFE'S FOLLY.

Life is said to be one thing after another.
First I'm hearty and then I smother.
Life jumps out between surprises,
but in the process wins no prizes.
I'm just a guy who's struggling along
to the tune of no special song.
Meanwhile, years pass and I'm not strong.
Age piles up my stubborn weaknesses
and weirdly turns into freakinesses.
My body's former youthful strength,
now lax, faces death at length,
so the whole battle collapses internally,
and misfortune rumbles infernally,
predictably confirmingly.

I DEPLORE THE END OF LIFE,
WHEN DEATH PUTS A POINT TO LATE STRIFE,
AND THE PUTRIFICATION IS RIFE.

When I have to say goodbye to life
to curtail its longevity,
I bewail its brevity.
Why did it speed up at the end?
That's an acceleration I can't defend.
Old age was anti-climactic
to my middle-aged burst of prime
when I was having such a great time,
when life was a lyric cascaded in rhyme.
Life is so sadly out of joint
when dying makes you miss the point.
Now I'm about to lose the whole deal.
Death climaxes life's late ordeal.
Why can't I squeeze in an extra meal
and give my stomach a belated steal?
Instead, I'm due to be skeletonic,
not recommended as a late-night tonic.
Life is too downright ironic,
voiced by a nightclub comic.
My brain turns into a lonely skull
piled empty, worse than dull.

THE INCONSISTENCY DIALOGUE

One time I'm happy, next time I'm sad. Why doesn't Life make up its mind?

Life's variable unpredictability is famously legion. You who've been living Life ought to have realized that truism by now.

I have. That's why I ask: "Why doesn't Life make up its mind?"

Because it's fickle when you want to stay happy, and consoling when you're too sad.

If it had a face, Life would be freckled with contradictions.

Life is always contradicting itself, from one minute to the next.

It's a jumble of inconsistency.

It doesn't even know the definition of constancy.

It ought to consult a dictionary.

The dictionary's contradictoriness would drive Life crazy. One page is different from the next, till you exhaust the whole alphabet.

The alphabet would entreat Congress for extra pages.

That bill would never pass. Congress is too conservative.

Then would language languish?

Enough to give wordsmiths anguish.

LOSING NOT ONLY LIFE, BUT FAME TOO. THAT'S THE VERDICT. WHAT CAN I DO?

Death kills me entirely,
putting me out of my fear
that had increased every year
till the actual showdown came
to end old age, so lame.
Life diminished in shame,
and even wiped clean my name
in failure of wished-for fame.
I lost to end my writing game.
Loss is purely enough. No more.
How redundant to calculate the score!

THE "FINISHING SOMEONE ELSE'S SENTENCE" DIALOGUE

Life keeps on moving along, till finally at one point Death gets irritated and suggests Life should hasten its aging to the point of satisfying Death's by now almost angry impatience to add another victim to his world record collection starting from Day One and continuing ad infinitum even beyond the present point of . . .

Time?

Yes. Thanks for concluding my almost interminable sentence that finally broke off at the end, but you rescued it just in . . .

Time?

Yes. How history repeats itself!

A DIALOGUE LIMITED TO WHAT'S INSIDE OF LIFE, ANYTHING ELSE GETS NO TREATMENT, HERE.

The reward of youth is sex; the penalty of age is death.

What did youth do to deserve its reward?

Getting born.

What did age do to merit its penalty?

Growing old.

How could youth help or prevent its birth and young state? How could age help or prevent its acquiring the later state?

Neither could help or prevent itself. No blaming, no faulting, upon them.

But within life, do actions count?

Yes, but only *within* it.

What's outside it?

What's not in it.

What's not in it?

The unaccountable. Ignore them. They're inconsequential.

Should I study what's inside life?

Confine yourself to that, it's still plenty.

And when I exhaust it?

Then you can see your way clear to other matters, Not *till* then, though.

A DIALOGUE THAT CURES DEPRESSION AND GIVES
THE KEY TO HAPPINESS. IT MAY CHANGE YOUR LIFE.
READ IT TO SEE IF YOUR CASE APPLIES. IF NOT,
THEN USE IT TO ADVISE OTHERS, SINCE IT COVERS A
MULTITUDE OF COMPLAINTS WITHOUT ELABORATING
ON ANY ONE POINT. FIRST TRY IT ON YOURSELF.
IF IT FALLS, THEN BE LIBERAL IN TREATING OTHERS
TO ITS WONDER-WORKING. DON'T EXPECT GRATITUDE.
GIVE, GIVE.

I'm depressed.

What about?

Life.

Well, you have nothing else to be depressed about.

Yes I do. Death depresses me, too, as a future "prospect."

But that's only part of life. If you had no life to be depressed about,
there wouldn't be anything for death to "matter" on. So your
depression is over-all, like a multi-vitamin pill that provides all
your nutriment needs in one capsule swallow. Since your depres-
sion spreads its scope over all generality in its inclusive sweep,

nothing in the particular need ever interrupt our cosmic preoc-
cupation. So cheer up. Your doom vastly precludes each separate
event, since the whole outgreats the parts. Bit by bit, nothings need
bother you. Life is one awful ache. But subdivide it, and you escape
the dread totality itself.

Thanks for your happiness formula. I'll go into simple gladness, of
which in the aggregate life's woe is a dreary compound.

AUTUMN REFUSES WINTER'S REQUEST
TO BORROW SEASONAL LEAVES IN PROMOTIONAL
QUEST.

Winter asked Autumn, "Please
leave me your remaining leaves
hanging barely from your emptying trees
in the seasonal hurried breeze,
a few to fortify my barren season
within the precincts of reason.
I'm so cold and forlorn,
I need a few reinforcements
to decorate my cheerless season."
At that, Autumn declined,
going on: "I want to publicize myself
at your frozen expense.
Thus your selfish request
for selfish reasons I must reject
in the Public Relations realm.
Let me be superior at the helm
in the rotation of our fellow seasons
in annual cycles as they roll
and along curved lengths carefully patrol.
I'm noted for my wonderful colors.
They're all mine. None may you have.

Substitute white snow
if you attempt to make a glow.
Leave my colors alone.
They're my crucial backbones
with their irresistible tones.
With their orange colored hues,
my superiority will cruise,
golden, causing you to bruise.
We must not be confused."

THE "REALISTIC DEATH" DIALOGUE

Innocently and ignorantly, I was given life at birth. That entitled me
to years: first to maturity and then to aging decay.

That was for the long haul.

Now I've gone through all that and am ninety.

Congratulations.

But I'm scared. I'm getting physically weaker and debilitated.

That's natural, at your age. But I can understand your fear of death.
That's a bitter loss of your whole deal.

(Breaking down in tears:) I love life and what it entails. Being dead,
all is lost. Religion mentions heaven. But common sense says
heaven is impossible and doesn't exist.

That's a realistic assessment. Sorry to rain on your picnic.

Death means skeleton and skull empty of consciousness and memory.

It sure does.

Why me?

Take your turn. Plenty have gone before you.

When it's my turn,
will I have to burn?

No, you won't feel a thing.

What satisfaction will *that* bring?

Simply not to be in pain
is considered by comparison a great gain.

From that consolation I can't refrain.

Then death has a better image?

I'd rather avoid its scrimmage.

THE "OF COURSE!" DIALOGUE

Life is an opportunity to enjoy yourself.

That's an optimistic point of view. Life is also a danger for being miserable.

Don't remind me.

It depends on the way you look at it.

Expectation doesn't always pan out.

Disappointment and frustration often defeat our initial wants.

Yes, wanting is a risk.

Nothing ventured, nothing gained.

What grains of wisdom we've learned to utter!

Yes, life is an experience compiler.
The older we grow, we become wiser.

But sometimes we become fools.

Is that the stuff of comedy?

Other people may convert the evidence as funny, but the victim doesn't necessarily see it that way.

No, so watch out.

I do, so as not to be caught napping.

We've got to be on our toes.
If not, look out for the woes.

Life is certainly opposed
by a miserable crew of foes
that trip you up any way
and defeat the object of your play.

MODERATION VERSUS EXCESS,
DEPENDING ON WHAT YOU PROFESS.
VARY YOURSELF, NEVERTHELESS.

Life goes from one thing to another.
If you have all at once, you smother.
So gradually ease everything out,
and vary your weight from thin to stout.
Be just as well even-tempered,
and of all clubs be a member.
Distribute yourself among people
as a denizen of society
and an advocate of propriety.
But occasionally go to town
with enough excess and extravagance
as to get revenge over moderation
by going full length to the other extreme
and live life as a bizarre dream.that trip you up any way
and defeat the object of your play.

PUTTING FAMILY PRESSURE
BY THE POEM THAT YOU USHER.
DOES IT REALLY GIVE THEM PLEASURE?
OR ARE YOU ONLY JUST A PUSHER?

Full force on the poem,
so don't let your attention roam
from the theme's specific location
in verbal sequence of station
along the pretty variation.
Then finally end this poetic piece
and show it to your nephew and niece.
They exclaim: "Oh Uncle, how nice!
Can you summarize it precise?
It's quite hard to understand.
Over all, were you really in command
with your wrinkled poetic hand?"

RELIGION IS THE LAST GASP
TO ELUDE DEATH'S FRANTIC GRASP.

Life tries to maintain itself,
but aging makes it harder.
This internal resistance
makes "giving up" the easiest way
to face one's exit day.
Your whole body drains its will
to be the guardian and the sentry
of life-protection.
"Easy come and easy go"
take on the lazy motto.
Extinction creates "blotto."
You're done for. That's the end.

The trail stops. Nowhere to blend.
Will your "soul" remain?
Sorry. Religion stops too.
It will no longer accompany you,
especially if you're not there
to fill its lungs full of air.

THE "IRRITATED RESENTMENT" DIALOGUE

(Characters: two old men.)

Life makes us love it, and then we get kicked out.

That's not fair!

Who are you to determine what's fair or not? You didn't make the rules.

It's anarchy. We're at the mercy of a tease. We get to love Life in spite of its innumerable flaws and setbacks. Then it abandons us to the nonentity of death. We're left in the lurch, without a perch.

Well, at least we did have it for a while.

And then to get abandoned! What a hoax!

Still, what little we got *counted*.

But it died out.

Well, we're still here.

Not for long.

Getting old was part of the game. Didn't you know?

Too old, and then death: that's a double knockout blow.

All you do is complain.

Why not? When there's so much to complain about, creeping out of the walls?

That's the way the bubble blows.

It's an iron bubble that smashes our face in.

You're too graphic. Relax.

No. If I relax my vigilance, the thug Death might bump me off.

Well, that's what he's there for. Right?

Wrong. We shouldn't be allowed to get killed.

Are you setting rules again?

No. They hit me in the eye.

Well, adjust your winking.

You mean "blinking."

Are you never content?

I'm not a grouch.

What a lie! Ouch!

THE "BAD FAITH ROUTE TO HEAVEN" DIALOGUE

I'm about to die of helplessly advanced old age that debilitates my resistance to senile ill health. But I can salvage some actual benefit from mortality by attaining the goal of Heaven.

To get there, you must have faith in Christ. Do you?

No. I'm an atheistic skeptic and disbeliever.

Then forget about your undeserved dream of Heaven.

But otherwise how else can I benefit by death consolingly by compensation?

You can fake it.

How to pull that off?

You've been an actor with many miscellaneous character roles dotting your lengthy career in stage, television, and movies. Acting is pretension.

Can't you pretend devotion to Christ?

Sincerely, no. But I'll cynically turn phony and pretend. I've earned it by my lifetime devotion to the acting craft.

Heaven's benefits would be enormous. Much better than realistic death's empty unconsciousness devoid of a functioning brain.

You're right. Here's for an afterlife of bad faith. Does Heaven include sexy women?

FRIENDSHIP IS SOMETIMES APART. THEN THEY RENEW IN A FINE ART.

Friendship is a precious jewel
where us two'll
be good mates on good terms
and breathe on each other good germs.
Thus our friendship is solid and firm.
If one is sick, the other moans.
If one falls, the other crawls.
We help each other out of scrapes.
But if we need privacy, we draw the drapes
and hide from each other, like sweet apes
who each climb a different tree
to allow the other to wander free
into the teeming forest at large,
not to clash in a sorry barrage.
Then we re-meet at the other end
and renew the greeting to our dear friend.

REMEMBER SO-AND-SO?
SHE WAS REALLY ON THE GO
AND PART OF THE GENERAL FLOW
IN OUR SOCIAL NEIGHBORHOOD

The people I know well are significant in my life
till they drop me or I drop them.
But still the times we had together
weighed prominent for a while
and we were well met at the time.
But people shift in circumstances
and take on different stances.
Sufficient for the time were the dances.
Acquaintances and friends enhance
the exits and the entrances
of society's light-seated adventures.
Memory preserves their pictures
in echoes that sustain solitude
in so many different habitudes
and a mixed selection of attitudes.
Hello and goodbye to these friends
in their big beginnings and sad ends.

OTHER PEOPLE IN YOUR LIFE
LIVE FOREVER DESPITE STRIFE.

Never should old acquaintance be forgot,
even though some friendships do rot.
Whatever transpired during that time
is mentally a little poem full of rhyme.
Forgetting her or him is an absolute crime.
So bear the impress of their memory
and forget their decline into enmity.

The warm feeling of amiability
is well within your heart's ability
of deep remembrance to never forget.
Was he ever a lovely person? You bet!
So keep him tightly woven in your net.
But let him loosely fall apart
in anger's garbage dump for a start.
Yet true friendship is often a fine art.
Tragic is the necessity to part.

CONDITIONS AND LIMITATIONS OF EXISTENCE
(Pretentious title)

Is being alive our greatest asset?

Sure. By the same token, being dead is our greatest liability.

Those are the most primary evaluations of human existence.

Sure. Following that, all other considerations are negligible.

Well, now that we've established ourselves, where do we go from there?

To comparative trivialities, like the weather and politics.

Let's not go there. They're beneath us.

That sounds snobbish of you. Little details are the daily substance of civilization.

You're right. Pardon me for being haughty.

Being modest brings us down to our true size.

That's about the size of it.

Now that we know our own dimensions, let's consider the world.

That's where we enter reality.

I can't bear too much of it.

Let's take it a bit of a time.

Even that much sometimes seems too much.

But we can handle it. We're adults.

We came out of having been children.

That's going back in time.

We've evolved from that phase.

We live life forward, and remember it backwards.

That's a dizzy way of participating in the past.

Memory needs the exercise
to philosophize and make you wise.

"DEFINING LIFE" DIALOGUE

What is it, to *live*?

I've been doing it all my life, and I still can't put my finger on the answer.

I have a clue.

What?

Living is activity.

Isn't it thought too?

Thought is *included* in activity.

That seems like a paradox.

Well, it's true.

That's very well thought out.

Life acts thinkingly throughout its duration.

I've been living through it.

Consistently?

I'm an example.

Of what?

Life as active interplay of thought.

That's me, through and through.

Let's keep on living a long time.

Sure, if we continually duck death.

Is death an activity?

Not for long.

Doesn't death just miss out?

So do I.

THE "WHAT'S LIFE?" DIALOGUE

Looked at a certain way, is life a miracle?

Yes, but let's not get mystical.

But calling something a miracle—isn't that being mystical?

In a way, yes. But what are the facts?

What do facts have to do with it?

To make it concrete and empirical.

Are you getting scientific?

No, just practical.

That makes it more actual?

Yeah. Closer to life.

Then what is life?

How do I know? I'm just living it.

Is that enough?

No. While living it, we also analyze it.

In retrospect?

Yes, sometimes immediate retrospect, right behind the event taking place.

Other retrospect is long after the event.

Like sweet nostalgia.

Or bitter.

If too bitter, it's no longer nostalgia.

Then what is it?
Something like regret.

Oh, don't remind me!

PESSIMISTIC LIFE'S SUMMARY
IS MORE WINTERY THAN SUMMERY.

I'm jealous of the young who screw each other,
while I in senior impotence needn't bother.
Besides impotence I have insomnia
which I sleep off, so life is sunnier
when I wake up in the golden dawn
and bless the very day I was ever born,
though life contains too much misery
to justify its sublime mystery
nor come to terms with tragic history.
I die when dizzy Death puts a fist in me
to drain my energy to a listless me
slumbering in Death's rocky stupor,
which by any evaluation can't be super.

SLIM BLOND

The opportunities you had long ago
are currently inaccessible.
For example, that slim blond who flirted with you,
but you didn't take advantage of,
is now beyond recall,
so you didn't benefit at all.
If you go seeking her now,
it's too late, she's dead,
and you're too old yourself
to carry on a love affair
and become half of a lusting pair.
You could stamp your feet with regret
that you didn't get
what you could have had.
You were a careless lad
to miss the chance to be exquisitely glad
in a wonderful glorious marriage,
instead of now, a bachelor so sad
that your lonely life awaits only death
instead of that slim blond bride
you lost in a waste of pride.

THE EMPATHY DIALOGUE

I'm ninety, therefore I'm eligible for death.

Well, don't be in a hurry.

Staying alive is a prime priority. But being ninety scares me.

That would scare anyone. It gives you a small margin, time-wise.

Time being not only a factor, but it's of the essence.

Use it wisely, and if possible, joyfully.

Well, joy is extreme. "Having fun" is a little more realistic.

Yes, that's a more moderate estimate for a goal, considering your age. Anyway, use your preciously shrunken time wisely for "having fun"'s sake.

Thanks. Your wish for me seems full of empathy, since it's identical with my own wish for me.

Then have double fun.

I'll set up a fund.

THE DEATH-FRIGHTENING DIALOGUE

How can I forestall my own death?

Worrying how little time you have left will only make its advancing approach all the more menacingly scary, as you start panicking in horror.

How can I be brave?

Only by resigning yourself helplessly to your helplessly advancing fate.

Is it inevitable?

Guaranteed. It's a big vast promise.

Can I slow it down?

Only by playing tricks with your mind.

Mathematical?

Anything artificial, in desperation.

Imminent death is pressing down on me. I can feel its cool breeze.

Does it contribute to your ease?

No. Fear and terror.

That's no error.

Being so scared how old I am drives me frightened of death.

Well, you ought to be. Your desperate plight is realistic.

Being a realist doesn't help, it makes it worse.

You're not only frightened *of* death, you're frightened *to* death.

Let's not go *that* far just yet.

Pay, pay, your ominous debt.

Are you sadistic?

No, just compiling your statistic.

THE "DON'T SCARE ME" DIALOGUE

My getting too much older is verging on a dangerous level of being uncomfortably close to death.

Then take steps to be prepared for that extremely reluctant possibility or rather eventuality.

Fear is gripping me.

Develop a counter-attitude of accepting your fearfully rising discomfort as being unavoidable.

But by accepting it, could I take perverse comfort in it? It's too grim.

Be hardened.

But that's not being "heartened."

They only *sound* alike. Don't be fooled.

I feel sorry for myself.

At least you're better off than being actually dead.

Don't scare me with grim reality!

It's not there yet.

That doesn't console me.

You're spoiled.

You're pitiless.

I'm only being realistic.

Only?! What a euphemism!

FROM THE CONCRETE TO THE ABSTRACT IS THE WAY OUR MINDS ACT.

Is life more than just one thing after another?

You made it sound too simple. Life is so complex, it's hard to figure out.

Have you tried? Analyzing it?

Its essence eludes me.

"Its essence" sounds like an abstraction. I'm referring to life in the concrete.

Then we should be talking architecture.

Why?

Because so many buildings are made of concrete.

But what of steel or wood?

That's another matter.

Is intellect applying abstraction to matter?

In essence, yes.

But architecture stands out.

Essentially it stands up.

Well, what you say stands up.

Thank you. I stand firm.

But buildings stay, while you squirm,
since death will abbreviate your term.
Buildings will be there when you die.
You can't compete with buildings, however high.
While death has taken you so low,
buildings take their stand and glow,
resisting winds that fiercely blow.

HEAR DEATH'S CHURCHLY CHIMES
TOLLING DOOM IN DEAD-RHYMES.

I'm old enough to die.

Congratulations on your longevity, which is due to end.

Rather than your congratulations, aren't I due for your consolations?

It doesn't matter. Away you go.

It's not a joy-ride.

No, you lose your hide.

In a deadly grave, reside.

END RHYMES
TO PAY OFF MY CRIMES

Death is a sad result
of mortality's prime insult.
Against it, you can't revolt.
It blasts you in one bolt.
So go to your euphemistic "reward."
"May it never come," was what I swored.
But I was asleep, and snored.
"Eternity's" arrival had me bored.

WOULD A QUICK BURST OF BREVITY
GIVE YOUR JOKE MORE LEVITY?
BUT NOT YOUR LIFE, WHICH WANTS LONGEVITY
AS OPPOSED TO BREVITY.

Life is the best thing going for me.
Defend it from adversity.
Protect it with all your might;
and if necessary, even fight.
Extend life to longevity.
Absolutely no virtue would be its brevity.
Much better resort to brevity
when telling a joke
(which might increase its levity)
and then with your elbow giving a poke
to an eagerly listening folk.
But brevity for *life* is no joke.
So dawdle out time before you croak.

DESPERATE PLOY,
TO NO AVAIL.
AWAY WE GO
TO "KICK THE PAIL,"
THOUGH WE STALL LONGER
LIKE A STUBBORN SNAIL.

Can I make headlines by being the first and only human who dodged death?

In a word, "no." I can understand your desire to be sensational. But you'd only inspire envy.

If envy includes jealousy's hatred, it's a price I'm willing to pay.

That avails you naught.
It can't even be bought.

It was only a self-sparing thought.

In death's snare, get good and caught.

Being the first exception was my desperate resort.

Sorry. No one is ever the sort.
Your ambition deserves everyone's snort.

HOW FAR CAN LOSS GO
TO EMPHASIZE YOUR BLOW?

Dying is the ultimate bad luck.
You lose the whole buck
along with the extra change,
and your finances are deplete
in your savings' lifetime defeat.
Your pockets and wallets are empty,
and your bank declares enmity.
This includes your Life Force
as well as mere money, of course.

A CONFESSION MADE TOO LATE
TO MAKE THE PUBLISHER'S DEADLINE DATE

I'm turning into a bones-&-skull
enshrined in a tomb so dull.
Away I go into the "hereafter"
that doesn't inspire peals of laughter.

A DRAMATIC DIALOGUE, TILTED TOWARD DEATH

Death erases all memories, even those of loved ones.

How could Death be so mean?

It just is. Its mean streak blocks it from accepting memories of
sentimentality and nostalgia.

Death seems like a cold bastard without compassion.

That's a great reason for avoiding it.

I appreciate your advice, but, being already "at Death's door" due
to extreme old age riddled with terminal disease, it's too late for
me even to put up a token struggle.

Well, it's "curtains."

Thanks for that theatrical metaphor. Were you in the theater?

Only as spectator.

Did theater seem to duplicate human life itself?

Sometimes exaggeratedly so.

How appropriate!

Melodrama sometimes seems *too* real.

Nothing is too real for Death to obliterate.

The monster has no respect for art.

THE "AT REST" DIALOGUE

Avoid Death if at all possible.

Of course. I'd be a dope otherwise. Every fool knows that, where Death is concerned, the only viable strategy is to avoid it.

But a lot of heroes don't.

Well, they have a real cause to risk it for, like their nation's honor.

Death is unrewarding.

A lot of posthumous medals are bestowed.

Yeah, but does it do the hero any good?

No.

My argument rests.

So does the hero.

Death is not a rest.

Yet it does arrest.

Oh, take a rest.

YOU CAN'T REHEARSE
THIS DEPARTURE VERSE.
THE REALITY IS WORSE.

Taking your last breath
is an invitation to Death
which the latter can't resist.
Weary old age did insist.
So people take your corpse away.
You can't return another day.
Sealed up in your tomb,
Life can never resume.

You've had your fun, so goodbye
under the sightless sky.
The sounds that thrum the world
the world has ceased to sound
to dead ears underground.
All the music whirls by
decomposed when you die.
You leave no soul behind,
and heaven is a myth
you'll never reckon with.
So goodbye forever
in your last endeavor.
Pity we must sever.
Your bones are strewn apart.
Death is departure art.
Resumption can never start
when dirty Death did its part.

AN OBVIOUS NON-PRIORITY.
OTHERWISE I DOUBT YOUR SOBRIETY.

If someone's dead, he's had it
and he's past it.
His value is useless,
putrid and fruitless.
Ignore his non-existence,
and confine your persistence
to vital matters only,
excluding the rotten dead
whose revolting condition
is unworthy your attention.
I'm sorry to even mention.
Death is no contention.

Concentrate on those on board
like yourself, who consume life's hoard.

THE "WEIRD MIRROR" DIALOGUE

Expecting to see myself reflected back, I thrust a trusting look into my usual mirror.

Then did your image take shape?

Oddly, no. Instead, an echo came out, deranging my senses from sight to sound.

Were you insanity bound? What explains this freak incident?

It must have been hallucinatory.

Have you recovered?

Looking again, I received my normal image, with the usual result automatically restored to place.

So it was a momentary aberration to get a sound echo when you earlier looked?

An inside job had made the mirror seem like a crook.

Have you confounded a conspiracy theory?

No. An occult cult wasn't responsible.

Then what explains that abnormality? Was it some kind of stunning stunt? In retrospect, what did your echo sound like? Therein would lie a clue.

It sounded like a ghostly wail from the unknown.

Enough to have your cover blown? What had you concocted?

A mystery inexplicable.

Maybe you're an imbecile.

§

An echo instead of an image?
What was this aberration's lineage?
Did it emerge from inside the mirror's uncanny interior?
Or were my weakened sight and hearing inferior?

OUTWITTING DEATH TO GET TO HEAVEN

I'm so years-redundantly old. My body is over-ripe to die. I can't hold out.

You sound the note of terminal desperation.

Yet I have a recourse.

What could it possibly be? A medical miracle?

No such luck. It's the religious consolation of heaven.

But that's unscientific, since sober common sense assures us that heaven has never existed.

Despite science's rigorous support of common sense, I rely on the religious invention of a "soul" to contradict the harsh reality of death's vacant emptiness of unconscious non-cognition.

You're crazy.

My extreme bodily decrepitude permits me the desperation of faith.

I'll plunder that miracle.

You ought to have your head examined.

They already examined my entire brain-body and pronounced me metaphorically at "death's door."

It will slam right in your face with a burst of emphatic finality.

Not quite. My loose brain having turned into hard-headedness, my new skull will resist the door's thudding slam to keep it ajar for hope's grace to sneak back in.

Not without using your knob.

PRELUDE TO THE END
TURNING ROUND THE BEND

Life as I "know" it is no longer here.
It's precious, lovely, and dear,
but old age has put a blot on it,
to make it no longer fit
in reality's larger scheme.
So say goodbye to the dream
that was implicit to your prime
but no longer holds, this time.
Old age is the culprit
that leaves us thrashing in this pit,
having arrived at wit's end
to senility's disastrous trend
that increases by and large
to death's final barrage,
that signals a terminal case
of the card player having lost his ace.

EVOLUTION'S EXTENT
TILL NOTHING MORE IS MEANT?

First, love leads to lust.

No. Lust leads to love.

Doesn't it vary in each case?

The circumstances differ, but reproduction gets served, for babies clamoring to get born, to improve their status from mere embryonic shrimp to ultimately fully developed maturity and then steady decline into old age's precarious adjacency to death's final horror.

Well, that's life.

Is that all?

Each species member is allowed one life at a time. When time is up, that's it.

That's all that evolution can yield?

You expected more?

I'll go see, and explore.
(*Leaves, then returns.*)

Well, what did you find?

The marvelous majesty of body and mind.

THE "BIG SPLASH" DIALOGUE

I've developed a severe tremor in my right hand, so that trying to eat soup with a spoon turns into a splashing event.

You can invite spectators by selling them tickets to that "splashing event."

No. I won't exploit my infirmity. Calling attention to my increased old age would only invite sympathy.

Well, if sympathy leads to compassion, you'd revel in people's compassion.

Instead of compassion, I could inspire pity for being old.

That's the same thing.

But if people feel sorry for me, it could lead them to contempt and its attendant mockery.

That would make them cruel. So don't expose yourself by tremoring with soup, thus splashing it. You draw foolish attention.

Now I'm too self-conscious, thanks to you.

Developing an inferiority complex?

I've already demonstrated that. I want to rebound and get dignity.

If you fail, you'll be self-indignant.

THE "MIRROR" DIALOGUE

Do you frequently reflect on life?

I resort to it for material to contemplate upon.

Life inspires thought?

Without thought, life would be self-ignorant.

Does that include innocence in the bargain?

Of course. Innocence is child-like ignorance.

That's charming and sweet.

I used life as a mirror for self-reflection.

How did it work out?

Amazingly, instead of getting a self-image from the mirror, I got a self-echo.

You mean your heard yourself instead of seeing yourself?

On reflection, yes.

Was the *mirror* strange? Or *you*?

That requires self-investigation.

No. Investigate the company you bought the mirror from.

But I didn't buy it. It came with the house I rented.

The mystery deepens. Consult the landlord.

He doesn't speak English.

Get a translator.

You're too demanding! How far can we go?

I got energy from recent sleep.

I'm the opposite. I'm sleepy.

Then is this whole scenario being dreamed by you?

How do I know?

Then consult the mirror.

I'll do that, and study the feedback.

LIFE'S DAZZLING BUT CONFUSED PUZZLEMENT

Life is what you make of it.

We don't have that much control. We drift into circumstances and then face limited adjustment possibilities to make the most of.

So life throws us here and there?

We just have to ride along with it.

Well, it sure is a learning experience.

I'll never get over it.

But you're in its midst. Lift up your paddle.

It's too wet and gets heavier.

Plow on.

That's on land. Are we mixing metaphors?

How can we not, life being such a mixed bag of infinite miscellany?

I'm going sheer nuts.

Nuts come in many varieties. Which?

GETTING OLD HELPLESSLY

Getting old is a big handicap.

What can we do about it? Wish we were young again?

No, that's futile. Let's just accept the handicap and get on with it as best we can.

But the handicap grows worse, even as we speak.

So it be, adding to our struggle. Just gather our failing strength and keep resisting.

But leading where? Where will it ever end?

It's in death's direction.

Can't we reverse it?

Are you crazy?

Then we plow on?

There's no other choice.

But won't failing health arrive straight smack into death?

It's inevitable. But we have no choice.

I can't bear where we're bearing.

It's no fun, that's for sure.

Well, we're in for it.

Will we get out alive?

Sure. Do dogs bark?

DEATHBED DIALOGUE

I'm on my last legs, horizontal in my death bed, having been administered morphine. So goodbye, it was great to know you.

You too. Must you go?

It's that drastic. Yes.

I'll remember you, but you'll be dead enough not to return the compliments.

Sorry. I feel guilty to be so neglectful, but death is a hard task-master.

I apologize in advance for my enforced forgetfulness of you.

You're really not to blame. I can't hold you to remembering me, since death grants no favors.

If possible, I'll try to forestall my impendingly imminent death by a few last-ditch minutes, to be able to re-live the old times we used to have together in nostalgic revelry.

You were a real pal. But better me than you, in the choice of who's surviving.

Now I'm angrily envious of your being the survivor and me being the dead one. I wish it could have been reversed.

Don't begrudge me life. Isn't it consoling that at least one of us remains to keep our shared memories alive?

No. I'm resentful.

Then drop dead.

EATING BEFORE DEATH

Does death create religion?

The *fear* of it does. We'd resort to anything to escape the horror of imagining ourselves in the non-existence of nothingness unalleviated by consciousness and personal identity.

What strategy does fear advocate?

The possibility of something beyond anatomy like a "soul" bringing you to something called "heaven."

What an idea! Worth trying.

Is necessity the mother of invention?

It sure is.

But what if it's an illusion?

Defy that with forced belief.

What if it doesn't work?

The horror of this negativity can't be stomached.

But food can be.

No meal can be too substantial, in this crisis.

Is it an exit-stential crisis?

Everything is at steak.

Well done? Or rare?

I'm not fussy. But lavish some mustard.

But what about ketchup?

I can never "catch up" with my youth.

Now we're beginning to burp out the truth.

LOYALTY TEST

(Visiting old friend on death bed.) How are you?

If I try to kill myself, could you please prevent me?

To thus intervene would put too much responsibility on myself, which I refuse to do.

It's my last request. How could you refuse?

Because, contravening your will and wish, I'd like to keep you alive.

But why? Considering my frail health and devastatingly advanced age have reached death's danger point of imminent immediacy?

Pushing your own panic button on me, despite our longstanding and mutually loyal friendship, reduces me to dithering incapacity and hence absolute refusal.

Thanks. I was fooling you by testing your loyalty. I'm relieved you refused.

I wouldn't betray you.

Good. Now that you're here, make yourself comfortable and we can talk at leisure. Have a drink and just ask my medical aide to give you food. Prolong your welcome visit.

Sorry, I can't stay. I have another appointment. Take care. *(Leaves.)*

Was he a true friend?

THE INCOMPLETE ARGUMENT, HAVING BURST TO AN UNDISPUTED STOP

How do you feel about living?

Are you crazy to so ask me? "Living" is so broadly obvious a tricky proposition, that it's unanalyzable.

Then what's philosophy for?

Getting our bearings. Feeling the weather.

If living is feeling and doing, then can we can put the spotlight on it and narrow it down to the component parts?

Are we discussing psychology?

If we're not, we're bearing pretty close to it.

Look, I'm tired of this kind of talk. Which one of us is the crazy one?

Don't look at me.

Are you accusing me? If so, of what?

Don't insinuate.

Look who's talking.

This is going nowhere.

Let's follow it.

ABANDONMENT

Now that you're dying, life having reached a critical point of imminent death's almost instantaneous immediacy, could you quickly look back on your whole life and come up with a final conclusive analysis of it?

No. My brain isn't working so well.

Try anyway. Be my guest, so guess away.

Well, it seemed long, with many intertwining paths.

Proceed. You're doing well.

My memory is failing.

Well, that's in keeping with the rest of you. Keep trying.

My whole life was pointing to this very minute.

But what about all the good times you had?

They're being overlooked, since the spotlight trains itself on this climactic scene of throbbing immediacy.

So you're betraying the good old times you had?

No, just turning my back on them.

Well, you've "had it." Good luck.

Good luck!? I'm going beyond "luck."

Whatever. Never mind that I asked.

Are we being terminal now?

Speak for yourself. I've got to hurry. I've got an appointment. *(Leaves.)*

(To himself:) Well?! What nerve! Being abandoned, neglected. Maybe I wanted too much? Some sympathy and sorrow?

BEING IN THE MIDDLE BETWEEN OPPOSING APPROACHING FORCES

How's life treating you?

Not too well. It's allowed me to lose my vigorous prime and maturity, through that agency of *time*.

Can't time slow down?

That's my subjective request for personal advantage. But how can I stop running out of time, with its irresistible wastage?

It's not waiting to take orders from you. It goes at its own pace.

But I'm being lost as Death approaches.

Time goes in one direction, Death in the opposing direction, both bearing down on you.

Having those two adversaries is enough to crush me, in a pincer movement.

Well, it's not *your* fault. Obviously, like rival women, they have a crush on you.

In vain. I reject both.

Still . . . they have their way with vulnerable men like you.

I'm trying to practice being elusive.

With those odds, you need *luck*.

Where is it available?

It's intangible.

That's no help.

DEATH'S STARVING APPETITE

Is my lengthening past gradually building up to a climax?

If you call Death a climax, yes.

My past has grown too vast. It so dwarfs my shriveling future, that obese gigantism is threatening to virtually overwhelm my microscopically tiny future that a magnifying glass can't detect.

That contrast of length is your doom's knell.

The clashing one-sidedness is splashed over with Death's salivating for his full meal ahead.

Yet, it consists of Life's meager left-over.

Death has always been a scrounger. It doesn't rest on ceremony. It's just a bare-bones scrabbler.

THE "NOT FEARING DEATH" DIALOGUE

Now that I've reached such an old age, is the time ripe for fearing death?

Go right ahead. Now or never. You may die before starting your fear.

I'll start now.

Why were you abnormally slow? Most old people start fearing much earlier.

I guess because life was good to them enough to value it.

But not in your case?

I was always poor and wretched, had no talent to get a good job, and women never loved me.

Those are cogent reasons not to fear death, which now feels like a refuge for escape from a disappointing life.

Yeah, but I can never come back again.

That's all right. It was bad enough the first time, as you innumerated.

But I thought my luck would change with rebirth.

What if rebirth turned out to be a different baby from you?

Good! A complete turnover!

TWO OLD MEN IN CONVERSATION

How's life going?

I hope it's not *going*. It's worthwhile to hang on to.

Sure, but it's coming at a reduced rate. My prime of youth and vigor and romantic ecstasy has drifted into the past, leaving me with life's dregs, at the bottom of the cup, like a used-up tea bag with the tea leaves scattered about, deserving to be called "dregs."

Yet you're still living, at reduced quality.

But without youth and its love fests.

Well, be content with less.

You call that living?

Though you're past your prime, you have the consolation of ripe nostalgia for the "good old days."

They were good old days, but these new ones stink. All they do is regret the passing of my own "golden age," that has turned into rusting lead flaked off into the wasted ozone and leaking pus.

But this is the age of serenity and being a sage.

A sage is a doddering old fool.

But these twilight years are full of mellow fruitfulness.

What a romantic you are!

Youth is a hard act to follow.

But being old is not to be a nobody.

Yes! You're still alive!

Where's youth?

Consult memory.

HE'S NOT THAT SPECIAL.

I want to slow up my living so I could live longer.

That's unnatural. Live at your usual rate.

But then I'll die sooner.

So be it.

You can shrug your shoulders about that. But it's *my* life.

Look, death is your destiny, so be a *man* and accept it.

But *women* die too.

That's irrelevant to you. Fulfill your destiny.

But it's ugly if it includes death.

It's a package deal. Life and death lumped together, one following the other in strict biological order.

But I'm a non-conformist.

You're also spoiled. It was all laid out when you were born. One to a customer. Standard life, followed by standard death.

I'm reduced to normality?

In *your* case, normality flatters you.

ATTEMPTING A LIGHTER MOOD

(Dialogue by Two Old Men)

Bad things happen to people who get old.

Yeah? What, for instance?

Death, for example.

You can't get any worse than that.

No, but you can stay alive and *still* suffer.

How?

Memory loss.

Well, it means you're going downhill. But at least you're alive.

Hey, this conversation isn't exactly merry.

No? Let's pull out of this grim impasse.

I'll do the honors. What did the mayonnaise say to the icebox?

What?

"Close the door. I'm dressing."

You expect me to laugh?

Well, it was fun trying.

THE UNNOTICED BIRD

The bird flew in nowhere's direction
till, out of sight, the wings stopped churning
and the motor idled on a distant tree,
and branches fluttered with the bird's motion.
On the ground, food was pecked into digestion
lightweight in gravity's mystery.
The bird's brittle body
packed up strenuous mileage
hopping on a journey from stop to stop
till the tiny automatic heart
ended an unrecorded life
watched by thousands of anonymous eyes
peering lost into sovereign skies.

PARANOID OVER-ANTICIPATION

Life is one damned thing after another.

Let it happen. I'm all prepared for any eventuality, even the unforeseeable ones.

Have you been through thick and thin?

Or anything else, for that matter.

Then you're in good shape.

I'm buoyant with confidence.

Let life do its damndest. What about surprises, which you can't easily foresee?

Then I'll take them on, and learn with improvising how to cope.

I envy you.

Don't. I'm also nervous, despite boasting being buoyant with confidence.

How can you reconcile those two opposites?

Inconsistency is my fallback position.

You need lots of that, to cope.

I'll use any method necessary.

Any?! Inconsistency consists of *every* expedience possible in the art of pragmatism.

Are our enemies so numerous?

No. The possibilities outnumber the enemies. Keep your paranoia within bounds.

If there's an argument, I let reality decide.

IMAGINING DEATH, PREFERABLE TO THE REAL THING

Imagining death is different than being dead.

So?

So don't slide off the edge into real death. Keep it on the mind instead of being in reality. The mind can waver, but reality entraps you forever, allowing no escape valve.

I'll follow that advice: keep death in the worry bracket instead of enveloping you in earnest.

That advice could save your life.

I'll follow it for dear life.

THE "DIALOGUE" DIALOGUE

Is the world the best place for human life?

That's my assumption. If it's not, then people have to adjust, to get into approximate harmony with the world. "World" and "Life" take on an ongoing alliance, and rough each other over, back and forth.

Thanks for sharing your suppositions.

What are yours?

Pretty much in the same ballpark as yours.

Are we in league? Are we the same person?

We *are* in league. But we have to be two different people to call this a dialogue we're engaged in.

Sure. I have a different voice.

And vice-voice-a. We take our turns.

Now it's yours.

Let's keep rhythm, without falling over.

THE MASCULINE FAULT OF GETTING TOO OLD

The older I get, the less women seem to welcome my inappropriate advances.

I can't blame them. At eighty-five years old, you're not a prize for women's later crop of recently born beauties.

I become less and less a suitable contemporary of juicy young women plump in haunches and breast?

That's a fair assessment. Nature ceases to be your ally. You're grotesquely wrong-aged as a candidate for seduction.

I might as well be dead.

Hush! Nature might be listening and taking a hint.

HUMOR DEGRADING DEEP SENTIMENT.
IS COMIC RELIEF NECESSARILY FUNNY?

Being deprived forever of a long, long loved one gives Romance a melancholy reputation it can never shake off with that tragic ending of intolerable loneliness.

That very statement makes me want to weep forever, in tears of deep sentiment, often derided as "sentimentality."

At what point does simple deep sentiment become hopelessly sentimental?

At the point my tears drench the front of my shirt in layers of staunchy wetness through and through.

Did you say *starchy* wetness?

Oh, stop being materialistic, when sentiment is the very point.

Scientific measurement shouldn't degrade the quality of pure sentiment staunchly emotional.

We're attempting to make humor of an innately serious human matter.

That's because, after taking the poignant pill of tragic melancholy, we savor "comic relief."

Humor washes down serious misery by taking it apart and making fun? What sacrilege!

It's necessary mercy. Poignancy is too unbearable at length.

At what length?

I get no catharsis. You're not funny.

JACK AND JILL

When Jack and Jill
were "over the hill,"
they were too old to come back.
The world experienced their lack
and mourns their absence
from the nursery fraternity.
They disappeared into eternity.
Only in old books do they remain
the true Jack and Jill of childish fame.

HOW MUCH YOU HAVE LEFT?

Life is distributed one to a customer?

Yes, that includes birth up through your entire process.

Then once it ends, that's all you get?

Yeah. Then you have to face the music.

Death is musical?

Sounds like a dirge.

Well, wipe your tears.

But you have time left.

But I'm counting less and less.

Well, it whittles down.

It's experiencing shrinkage.

Down to invisibility?

No, leave some breathing room.

THE CONTROL FREAK'S COMPLAINT

I'm frightened that I have to die some time eventually.

Shouldn't inevitability calm you down? It's beyond your control.

That's the rub. I'm a control freak.

Then if you must control, then control your fear, since you can't control death.

Why is death so mean?

You're a cry-baby. Be a man!

That's the rub. If I'm a man, I must die.

Then be a woman.

Too late. At my advanced age, I'm too old for a sex change.

But add women to death. They're not immune.

Is there any immunity whatever?

Death is immune to its own demise.

That doesn't console.

Then practice self-control.

Is that my consoling role?

SOLITUDE'S CONCLUSIONS
AGAINST RUDE INTRUSIONS.

The poem rose in the mind but failed in the writing.
Crumbled up, it joined the debris
of the garbage can's unsavory sanitation.
The poetic mind recovered from the blow
and by internal advice
lay low, shut out from words,
joining the routine of pure unfocused thought
vaguely mixed between hunks of memory
and plans for the glittering future,
a raid against rumblings
of time's warning to hurry up –
for what? "Before it's too late."
Do the job that waits.
Don't put it off.
But it's only semi-urgent.
Life has done its duty anyway.
Take complacent joy in that.
Don't pile up pressure.
Past ambitions did their work
and brought me up to here.
Join it. You're being cheered.
You've escaped what you've feared.
The path that's cleared is now yours alone.
"Soul-searching" has brought you home.

WHAT HAPPENS IF YOU FORGET?
THEN YOU LOSE OUT ON SOME BET.

Memory depends on a previous event
which gives you something to remember.
The event qualifies you to be a member
of the fraternity of rememberers
who can recall a definite event
that once happened in your very life,
so that in your head you recall it,
since by experience you befell it,
so now you're able to tell it.
But later amnesia might quell it.

MEMORY'S LIMITED CAPACITY

Should old friends be forgot and never brought to mind? Shouldn't
we drink a cup of kindness to their dear memories?

Sure, of course. But what if they were only mere acquaintances?

Include them too. Spread the wide generosity of your gratitude to
all those who entered your life, except the ones your favor didn't
approve of for the honor of inclusion.

My life being so gregarious with multiple contacts, wouldn't my
inclusion width be too wide over the extent of so many years for
mere memory to carry such weight of sheer numbers?

True. So be selective and pick special favorites over time's vast
extent.

But wouldn't that reduction of selectivity preclude too many? What
disloyalty and failure of gratitude!

What mean bastards we are! Memory is too precariously finite,
except for prominent favorites.

So many that escape our justice!

Pity them. Who were they?

THE REGRETFULLY EARLY BORN

I'm mad at my parents and wish to sue them.

Why?

They mated too early to get me, so now I'm too old. If they had waited longer, I would be that much younger, and hence have longer to live.

That's a selfish estimate. Anyway, they're too dead for you to bother suing them. The judge would throw it out of court, and his colleagues would laugh themselves sick.

I don't wish to be a laughing stock, which would offend and compromise my dignity.

Why do you always think of yourself?

Why not? Self-love motivates me to improve my welfare whenever possible.

So you're an opportunist?

Yes, when the opportunity arrives.

And if it doesn't?

I look for something else to take advantage of.

FINALLY, A DREAM

Already dead a few years,
Jimmy Stagno eventually appeared
in a sudden dream I had one night

for my first sight, since he died,
of his true hallucinated form
that uncannily approximated the norm,
to my amazed surprise
that contradicted his demise.
There he was in front of me.
I was flabbergasted to silence.
He said no word, neither did I.
Seventy years marked our friendship,
but the shock woke me up.
But the dream screen lost him.
Now I was alone again
for nostalgia's resumption.
Real life undid presumption.
It was only a short sighting,
and reality won after fighting
to uphold logic.
There was no ostensible magic
of this ordinarily tragic.

THE ABSOLUTE WORST

Death is the worst thing that could happen to you.
It blinds you from any and every view.
It deafens you out of sound's range.
And all this negativity is without change.
So if possible, put off death
to the very last instant,
to preserve your life as long as you can,
independent of whether you're woman or man.
Once when you were a little child,
your parents trained you not to grow wild.
But death is worse than being tamed.

It's worse than every misfortune named
in whatever paper or book.
Robbing you of your life, death is a crook.
Curse on death for the life it took.
The absolute worst.
The most venomously cursed.
It never satisfies your thirst.
Any good, it makes to burst.

SOBERING REFLECTION

Life is only one to a customer? But what about divine rebirth in
Heaven of what's reverently called a Soul?

That's only a myth, to make religious observers feel less terrified by
impending death.

Surely mortality is defeated by strong Belief?

Don't be too sure. Lots of graves and tombstones feature under-
ground skulls and skeletons, with total loss of consciousness
throughout history's remaining time.

That's very sobering.

Even if you weren't even drinking?

EVERYBODY IS A ROBERT BURNS
WHO LIVES UPON MEMORY'S RETURNS.

I'll drink a cup of comfort
to old friends now dead
or else missing instead
with life still retained,
but address nowhere named.
Old acquaintances are less than friends,

but with some I still must make amends.
Whoever spoke from my past,
my dear memory will make them last
in slowed-down tempo, not so fast.
They come at me from all angles,
reminiscent of former entangles.
They're bright stars, or tinsel bangles,
shined upon by living memory
even if they're in the cemetery
and no longer reply to me merry
or by any means contrary.
I say to them, "Hello forever,
what happened on our last endeavor?"

MEMORY VERSUS ORIGINALITY

Does what we remember depend on what happened earlier?

Yes. A previous event or experience must precede the memory of such.

Then memory is dependent on what occurred originally?

Yes, it must be *based* on something.

So memory is a parasite?

Yes, it must be derivative.

Memory is only a mental image?

Yes, but it could be a distortion of the original.

So is memory intrinsically unreliable?

Yes, it could shift base or lose contact with the original.

It takes variation and loses connection?

Yes, unreliably so.

It takes imaginative liberty?

At devious variance.

So what good is it?

It's an ineffective compass; or sometimes a reliable guide.

Depending on what?

On its own auxiliary clause.

Are you crazy?

MEMORY'S HISTORY

Memory lacks the animation of the original event it's derived from.

The vivid primacy of experience is hard to replicate by deliberate or spontaneous memory images, which fall pale by comparison.

Memory is not a neat carbon copy. It vaguely recaptures some semblance of the original.

It's a stab into the past.

Does the past eke its blood, that crawls out over "now," turning redness into faded grey?

Please! Don't be so melodramatic.

But that's how life sometimes is.

Then we're movie stars, in feature roles.

Is this before the advent of technicolor?

Let's not be so old-fashioned. We're plunged so into the "now," we're creatures of the latest modernity, including unprecedented inventions of technical wizardry.

How long will *that* last?

Meanwhile, we crawl into old age and die.

Such anti-climax challenges credulity.

It's already jeopardized our security
and plunges us into obscurity,
memory fallen by the wayside,
having nowhere to reside.

SAD DIALOGUE

Life used to be full of youthful vigor and vitality, but after leveling
off, it's now a downhill drag into the precincts of death.

That sounds tragic.

It lacks redeeming magic.

Then submit to it. You have no choice.

I have no vote? I have no voice.

Succumb to your abysmal fate.
You can't regain your youth. It's too late.

Then pity me. I'm old.

It's out of place to appear bold.

I'm weak and helpless.

You poor old man!
In the horse race, you're an also-ran.

Tell bettors not to bet on me.
That will save them money.

They'll thank you and call you a honey.
So benevolent before you die!
Such character and personality!
You're a credit to our principality!

Thank you, my dear old friend,
for your precious wisdom at the end.

THE REMEDY-MANUFACTURING DESTRUCTION

The world is coming to an end.
Decay has begun to putrify
beyond what decency can defy.
"Too much" has done its deed
to push growth into weed.
The odds are against moderation
slowing down excess
that cuts life into pieces
and pulverizes mere matter
into thread-by-thread dis-tatter.
The rolling beast grows fatter,
consuming the grease left over
from hungry animals
that frighten their devourers.
So drowse out the last hours,
while the world skids away
from its planetary imbalance
on which we waste our talents
planning the collapsing palace
where dictators crumble at the throne
the nasty mob resents them to own.
The mob wipes away such remains,
and the final grotesque gorges on ugly stains.
Hilarious retards drown in the dusty rains,
leaving a puddle for new evolution
to create species that resist pollution.
Wait for it the next time,
as the world erases its crime.

A SEVENTY-YEAR FRIENDSHIP,
FROM BROOKLYN TO LONG ISLAND

The summer goes rolling by,
then another goes rolling by,
the illuminated clouds decorate the sky,
we played ball a lot
in old schoolyards,
with the sun following us.
Year turns out, year turns in,
school days come and go,
a friendship builds and builds,
it's solid, it's consolidated;
our Yankees won a lot,
we struggled with our poverties.
We walked to Coney Island
with a dog chasing us
that came out of nowhere.
Baseball was our love
that combined our heads.
Marriage now comes about,
in one case children too;
jobs alternate with play;
we played pool a lot
in senior centers
by our own improvised rules;
we ate cheaply in restaurants.
Age advances, still fun;
by now we've outrun the sun.
Our humor remained in old age;
now one of us dies,
giving the other wet eyes.
Goodbye Jimmy, I'll miss you.
His voice has rare stillness,

that out-talked me all that time.
I can never hope to catch up.

I'M DEATH'S DELICIOUS MEAL
WHICH MY CORPSE OFFERS AT A STEAL.

Death leaves me torn apart,
unable even to fart.
Death then has me to pick on
for a delectable meal
at bargain rate, a true steal.
Bones and all, I'm devoured
by Death's hungry appetite.
He holds me good and tight,
I unable to resist and fight.
I offer him delicious fare
with a recent corpse, extremely rare,
soft and juicy to the bone,
a whole meal for Death alone.
I'm devoured quite to a pulp
which Death finishes with a final gulp.
I sure was at Death's mercy.
He belches profound, as all can see.
Then I find myself inside
Death's now stout hide,
tickled by my recent corpse
that ran through Death's digestive course
with a plump thump, rowdy and coarse.
Then he turns me into manure,
the devoured meat juicy and sure.
He was on a diet, but this is no cure.

THE JOURNEY FROM START TO FINISH.
FIRST JOY, AND THEN THE GRIMACE.

Life is a free gift.
Hoard it with thrift.
But spend it with careless riot,
fiercely energetic, not quiet,
and all the passion you can muster,
before you ease off and rust her
as you go downhill and croak,
receiving self-decay as a joke
that explodes directly in your face,
and you lose your earthly place.
It was a great effort, but not sustained
when you had to relinquish your whole life's gain.
Your mourners weep with justified pain.
You gave such fun. Why couldn't you ever remain?

I OUTLIVED THEM.
DO THEY FORGIVE ME?

Memory releases youthful days
that were my glorious phase.
Dear old friends, you've been dead
and resound only in my head,
that endlessly plays you back again
to revive that ancient, ancient "when."
We played ball and ate together,
our conversation exceeding "the weather."
How am I still living?
I beg you to be forgiving.
As a survivor, I feel guilt.
Our friendships will never wilt,

so solidly were they built.
Those good old golden days of yore
empty my eyes of tears they pour,
rolling down my wrinkled face
and finally settling on my collar.
It's for your sakes that I holler.
We shared the essence of golden youth,
that never ceases to be our bracing truth.
Dear friends, you harbor the past.
And here I am, alone, aghast.
Nostalgia is a fine emotion
that brings everything back to motion.
But nothing can beat the days themselves
that are trophies only on my shelves.

WE SHARED GLORIOUS YOUTH
UNDER FRIENDSHIP'S REIGNING TRUTH.

The golden days are over,
when I used to be a rover.
I only remember approximations
of our old glorious stations.
You were my friends forever,
but now one by one you died,
and I alone survive,
full of helpless guilt.
Will our friendships ever wilt?
They were sturdy and well built.
But only alone in my head
will memory create you undead,
just the way you used to be
when we played and worked together, free
of all this nonsense of being apart

when, one by one, your deaths would start,
due to that spoilsport, old age,
that stopped our being on the same page,
which now is crinkled paper.
Here I am, wrinkled, alone,
unable to communicate, even by phone.
Any further dates we must postpone
into separate spheres, unknown
to our mentalities that used to be
sturdy, together, loving, free.

HOW NOT TO LET COMMON SENSE INTERFERE

How can I conquer death-fear, which increases the older I get?

Resign yourself to the inevitable, over which your only temporary solution is to stay as healthy as possible, with ever weakening results, till the very end.

That's unsatisfying.

Then what would suggest?

Going to heaven.

But you'd have to become *sincerely* religious.

At short notice? A crash course?

It depends on how soon you'll die. Begin your religious training now, immediately, when you'll have the most time left for safely beating (the deadline.)

All right. Does it include church attending?

Sunday is not enough. Go every day.

But common sense says that heaven is only a myth.

Take your chances by directly disobeying or overlooking common sense.

Then I'd feel like a truth fraud.

Pretend sincerity to obtain your goal, which defeats death.

Will my heaven residence seem under phony pretenses?

What does it matter? If you're there, you're there.

I guess the end justifies the means?

Yes. In time, your residence will accommodate your pretentious claim.

My rewards won't be ungainly, but heavenly, thanks to my flexibility, which underlies my impeccable character of good faith.

A VICTIM OF TIME, WHICH PERFORMS DEATH'S CRIME AGAINST YOUTH'S GOLDEN PRIME.

Life in its golden prime
leaves me far behind
my rate of old age
getting ripe for death's cage
to trap me after youth
matured beyond its truth.
So here I am, ready to die,
realizing that time *does* fly.
My mourners are too old to cry,
having forgotten the "me" they mourn,
since failing memory is their norm.

HOW I SERVE DEATH'S HUNGER,
WHICH INVADES ME LIKE A PLUNGER.

Death gets hungry when I'm about to die,
and salivates at my last breath.
I'm a new corpse ripe to eat
to appease Death's appetite complete.
He launches away at former vitals,
and eats what's left of my belly's titles,
that gourmets are ignorant about.
Devouring me, Death gets stout,
being inclined to excess fat
that promotes corpulence and all that.
He also drinks what's left of blood
that amounts virtually to a flood.
He's having such a jolly sup
that his dark morale rises up
to burp so hard and also belch,
being drunk on my former lungs.
The booze has been getting to him,
and he spits me out on a whim
from blood clots that spray on him.
My chances of revival are nil,
and he vomits me in one big spill,
signs to observe that he's probably ill.
Such disgust! But Death doesn't care.
He finds somewhere fresh air,
and unlike me, feels better already,
tired of proving himself obnoxiously deadly.
Meanwhile, I'm so dead,
he polishes me off like a piece of bread,
munching with teeth so brittle,
I'm all mixed up with his spittle.

IMPIETY
WHISPERED QUIETLY.

"Heaven is a hoax,"
I tell all folks,
but on the spot
I may be shot
by a lover of religion
with the brains of a pigeon,
who followed a "holy lord"
and swallowed the whole fraud.
Deception had been scored.
Accept a skull and bones
as tokens of death's moans
near the graveyard stones,
more credible than heaven
at the age of ninety seven.
So I'm an atheist
and make a glaring fist.
To be an agnostic
is to be too politic,
illogically slick.
Don't be a lousy phony
riding a crippled pony.

A LIVE LOVE AND ONE DEAD.
THEY BOTH GO TO MY HEAD.

to Candace Watt

I approximate understanding you
and try empathy too.
I sympathize and identify

with what you go through.
But still you're a foreign object,
yet I love you, you're mine.
How did we two combine?

to Jimmy Stagno

Jimmy Stagno was my friend
for seventy years, a long end
from early adolescence.
We laughed with words of eloquence
and loved to play baseball,
later pool, and loved each other,
riding in your car and walking,
and always talking, but now
you're the dead one. Where am I with you?
You were so real. Is it true?

OPERAS DEALING IN TRAGEDY
ARE LISTENED TO WITH EAR-BUILT STRATEGY.

to Jacob Smullyan

Life is inherently tragic.
Becoming dead is no magic.
No wonder operas, to be dramatic,
lead hero or heroine to doom
and spread the audience with musical gloom.
Loaded with suspense is the plot,
and first there's hope for heroine or hero.
The culmination builds up to zero.
Glorious arias are sung,
but the stars are shot or hung,

giving the audience a fit of tears
that internally weep for many years.
Plots conveyed as operas
are sold in albums, so shop for us.
So even at home we hear such songs
as musical delight eternally prolongs,
often morally dealing with rights or wrongs.
Opera is bound to give you a lift.
But if bored, then in your seat you shift,
and seem apparently miffed.
Keep your ears in good shape,
to listen hard with mouth agape.
But you don't have to pound your feet:
With the given opera, you needn't compete.

SOLITARY FLIGHT

The bird flew in, the bird flew out.
What's his itinerary all about?
Is he lost from his herd
or flock, that little bird?
Did he skip a beat in the migration
and digress from all his mates
who were flying through seven states
searching for a shore
to put down and build a nest
for further warbling from their fluttering chest?
Eggs must hatch
for this sole wanderer to greet his match
and start off again from scratch.
High aloft, the wings beat
before the return journey and retreat.
By sheer instinct, this surviving bird

has skies to go before he's heard
to get in his note and the last word.
Eventually he must die
and lose his place in the open sky.
The clouds will mourn the loss
of this lone wanderer.
He had a love and was fond of her.

TRAGEDY INTO FAMILIES' FRIENDSHIP. IS THAT AN EXCUSE FOR DEITY WORSHIP? OR IS THAT JUST A MORALISTIC SLIP?

A bicycle strayed from its path
and knocked down a pedestrian
who struck his head on the asphalt.
It was the bicyclist's fault,
or maybe the unaware victim's.
Let me criticize this transportation system.
The bicyclist paid for the funeral,
and the two grieving families
became unlikely friends,
to make a humanity of these ends.
Is that too sentimental? It depends.

THE INCONCLUSIVE ARGUMENT WITH A CONSERVATIVE ENDING, WITH NEITHER SIDE BENDING.

For everybody, life goes from one thing to another.

What a profound statement!

Stop belittling me with irony reinforced by sarcasm.

Your vacant clichés are wastefully irresponsible.

You reprimand me purposelessly.

Let's stop this bickering. If you're stupid, just say so, so we could quickly remove it from the agenda.

Oh, you have everything planned out already?

Yes. Why does everything have to be to your liking?

It doesn't. You're so misguided that you aim your ammunition fruitlessly at yourself.

Well, I'm protecting you from being in harm's way.

Your logic is tear-able up-able.

Let's split it down the middle.

No. I need the advantage.

Then you need it because you don't have it.

There's lots of things I need though already having them.

Then your greed is based on insecurity for what you already have.

They're worth protecting, by repetition.

If something good is what you already have, then keep it that way.

Your key is conservatism. But what if you don't have what you conserve?

Stop enigma-fying me.

I will if you follow suit.

I don't follow a suit. I only follow women.

No wonder they avoid you.

CELEBRATION AT LIFE'S END
OF EVERYONE WE CALLED A FRIEND
OR ONLY A MERE ACQUAINTANCE,
WHILE LIFE EBBS OUT THE FAINTEST.

All we have are memories
when life is nearly ended
of all the wonderful people
we luckily befriended.
So let's create a tribute
and wear your best old suit
to friends in our wonderful past
who joined us in the blast.
We'll review the entire cast!

LOVE UNREQUITED
CAN'T BE IGNITED.
HOW CAN YOU FIGHT IT,
ESPECIALLY AT SUCH AGE
THAT QUALIFIES YOU AS A SAGE?

Love is a good emotion to have,
provided it's requited.
So ask your loved one,
"Please give me a sign
that your love will equal mine
in ferocious intensity
to its full immensity."
But she replies,
"You don't inspire me to passion
in your obsessive fashion.
I now reject you,
though I respect you.

Find love with another lady
(even one too shady)
if you can, with your age of eighty:
whose numerical years are too weighty
to support your physical body
to have any lust that's hearty."

MENTIONING MY DEMENTIA
IS A MEMORY-LADEN VENTURE.

Being old, I forget things,
with senior dementia.
I forgot who I was,
but by looking at my fingers
I remembered by association
whose valuable fingers these are.
So then I recaptured my bearings
and took stock of me and the *world*,
which is my planetary residence
as a semi-geometric globe,
unless I'm an astro-phobe.
I remembered my first name,
but the last one escaped
after tantalizingly teasing me
with near-misses. Was I "losing" it?
I guess I'm near the end.
Death won't remind me of anything worldly.
Maybe religiously I have a chance
to enter "heaven" for a jig or a dance
with an angel or two, and then wrap it up
and enter emptiness for a spell,
with nothingness on which to dwell.
Anything—but *anything*—is better than "hell,"

if what I've heard is true.
But what can you believe these days?
Hell is only a rumor?
It's the whole world's tumor!
Do I sound dogmatic?
I'm self-autocratic.

DEATH AND NON-DEATH
ARE TWO OPPOSITES.
THAT'S WHERE THE ARGUMENT SITS.

Being dead is no picnic.
All the fun you can't have!
Death is the ultimate depriver
of what you wanted or wished for.
"You can't have this and you can't have that!"
is Death's constant taunting refrain.
It also denies you of a chance to complain.
So avoid Death if at all possible,
with your very life at stake.
Death prevents your meal of vegetables and steak
to appear on your very willing plate.
With all that very negative attitude,
you can't accuse Death of being a mere platitude.
It's real! So real,
it's beyond your ability to feel.
(What is feeling, anyway?
It has to do with the senses?
"We need it" is the general consensus.)

THE FORGETFUL STATE,
WHICH I CAN'T REMEMBER HAVING BEEN IN.
I MUST HAVE, BUT WHAT DO I KNOW?
MY BRAIN IS PRETTY DULL,
IN A PERENNIAL LULL.

Being old, I get forgetful.
I even forget what I forgot.
I don't remember what to remind myself of.
I should have tied a string around my finger,
but I forgot which finger.
This puts me in a vulnerable position,
with frailty akin to being on death's verge.
At that rate, I have an urge
to do myself in.
I've packed my things and stored them in a bin.
But *which* things? *What* bin?
I'm just a "forget" machine,
which functions so automatically,
I'm living virtually autocratically;
but I can't obey myself,
since I'm a rebellious citizen
with no zest for obedience.
Instead, I coast along on expedience
to make the end justify the means:
which I believe, by all means.
But am I really convinced?
I once was, but then I winced.
Now I'm not so sure,
and stare into the sky's azure.

THE ONE-WAY STREET
TOWARD WHAT'S COMPLETE

Life is a one-way street
unambitiously to Death.
Walking is just falling forward.
But the next, and then the next, step
places you in an awkward position
where Death offers its untempting proposition
to declare you an eligible candidate
to meet up for an unromantic date
for life at length to culminate
with its own loss, a terrific sacrifice
that depends on the ultimate throw of dice
for earth to move aside and make room
for your arrival, empty of gloom
or any other emotion
in the stillness of lost motion.

REMAINING MEMORIES
IN THE SKY'S STIFF BREEZE

The clouds grazing over the sky's blue meadow like stray cows
regale my remaining years with lazy old memories.
That drift of memories will turn softer
as death arrives with its persuasive offer
to drive the clouds into a woolen state
to pack me downward in my crate.

DEPARTING LIFE AT NINETY,
NEITHER DEEPLY GRAVE NOR FLIGHTY

Becoming ninety invites summing up
of how your longevity sprawled out
into pleasure, pain, and other things.
What variety life brings!
My life was filled and stuffed
to flood over the brim,
given both to calculation and whim.
Now my vision is darkingly dim,
as old age tampers with death's edges
and eliminates all previous pledges.
Down I go into the grave
with consequences not trivial, but grave.
Damned little from former life that I can save.
I conclude that I was neither an angel nor a knave.
So goodbye to the big bold world.
By social media was it unfurled.
All this knowledge I stagger with,
as I estimate life's broad length and width.
Now I number among the dead,
because my jaws are open but I can't be fed.

LAST EFFORTS, IN A PULSE BEAT

"Keep cancer-free; avoid heart attack or stroke; steer away from accidents."

Those are excellent warnings for self-preservation.

I heed them. Survival and longevity are my goals.

For how long?

Till old age does me in.

You're already wrinkled. Are you scared?

I'm addicted to living as a desperately urgent habit.

But you've obviously slowed up.

That's how time has been damaging me.

Yet you withstand its blows?

I'm desperate. But tired. I fear giving way.

Time has advanced too far. You're no longer in a comfort zone, which recedes from your fading visibility.

I'm momentarily desperate. Pardon my panting.

It seems faint, by now.

Keep hearing it.

MODERN GENDER

(Dialogue between two men)

If someone dies, and then I get born, does that mean that I replace him?

Not necessarily, because it may be that the one who died was a woman; and you're not allowed to replace *her*.

I'm not qualified because I'm a male, which only another female can replace the woman who sadly passed away?

Precisely.

Who installed that silly rule? Nowadays some public bathrooms are multi-gender. So why can't "birth-replacing-death" ease its old puritanical rules?

You're right. Modernity has got to be respected.

If history goes on, we have to keep up with it?

Yes. Going backwards is fatal.

That's in our genes since being natal.

Evolution is very particular.

In general, it is.

You can't fool around with it.

At your own risk.

TOO LATE FOR SALLY
IF WE RELENTLESSLY TARRY

I appealed to Sally
to help me rally
from being in the doldrums,
by being able to march to different drums.
Any embrace that she could afford me
would not in any sense have bored me.
Clutching the soft body of Sally,
whether on a high hill or deep valley,
would constitute the highest thrill
while gratifying the sexual will.
But alas, she's not available.
Already married, she's unassailable.
So I must keep my hands to myself,
and dream her as a trophy on my shelf.
Maybe one day she'll divorce
and give herself. So no need for force.
She'll serve herself up with alluring sauce
to make the climax more delectable
if I'm not too old to be susceptible.
To waste Sally by old age impotence
would be time's fault by coincidence.
To have Sally just before expiring
is bound to prove so fatally tiring.

JUDGING QUALITY

Life is not what it used to be.

Why not?

My youth and middle age are long gone. So what's left is merely my pre-death old age.

At least you're still living, so why complain?

It's a matter of quality.

What does that have to do with it?

Youth and middle age had better quality than my current old age.

Who are you to judge?

Who else, you fool?

GOODBYE'S SADNESS

Death is coming to my life,
but I don't know the exact date.
I live in fear, at any rate,
that death will catch me unaware
in its nasty universal snare
before I'm ready to say goodbye
to my old occasional pals and such,
with whom lately I'm not in touch.
I loved to have such a social life
to keep my loneliness tucked inside
on the thrilling, uneven ride.
My friends are closed up in memory
till they're all released
at the tail end of my tenuous lease.
How wonderful to know all of them!

Now another new generation
covers my coffin in ignorance
of what I once knew and lost.
That's how death has me bossed.
What I had is so easily tossed.

WHICH CONVERSATIONAL PARTNER

(Which conversational partner has the advantage over the other, in his terse response?)

Life is one thing after another.

Oh, you're so profound!

Stop your sarcasm. At least I wasn't pretentious.

No, but you were simplistic.

You mean I was stating the obvious?

To a boring degree.

You're so critical!

You give me a lot to criticize.

Must everything be an opportunity for you to comment on?

I like expressing my reactions.

You seem to have a busy head, like a bee's hive.

Now you're being metaphoric.

It was only a simile.

Give yourself credit.

I do. I don't need your advice.

Are you being contentious? You seem irritable.

I get tired talking to you.

Then stop, then.

No. You stop first.

Are you greedy to have the last word?

Yes, but my intention was not to impress you.

It was to get the better of me?

We're not fighting.

Then why am I defending myself?

WHAT'S LIFE?

What's your attitude toward life?

Live and let live.

That's your *social* attitude. I'm referring to your private individual attitude.

Be glad you're here, and try to prolong it.

So you're here for the long haul? Is longevity your aim?

Sure. Life is fun for the most part, despite being a pain in the ass at times.

Life is for what you could get out of it?

That implies selfishness.

Why not? Aren't you Numero Uno for yourself?

Yeah, but I want to share the riches. My fellow others count too.

I never heard such generosity.

Don't be sarcastic.

We're all in this together.

That's both social and individual.

Those are the two bi-components of life.

Cutting the pie into slices?

Don't be cleverly metaphorical. Life is serious.

Should I get into a crying fit over it?

Only at the end.

Leave-taking is a weeper.

Wipe off my tears.

They'll only start flowing again.

Then keep wiping.

Let me know when life is just itself.

At all times, it always is.

How does death come into it?

It doesn't. It's separate.

That's the trouble.

ATTEMPTS TO UNDERSTAND COMPLEXITY'S HAZARDOUS RELATIONSHIP WITH COMPROMISED SIMPLICITY

What's life's essence?

If life were champagne, effervescence would be its essence.

You're frivolous, like a bunch of bubbles that attack each other and break in the effort. Define life, if you will.

It's that which keeps us alive.

Stop playing around with words. Turn serious.

Life is one thing after another. Is that orderly enough?

What about simultaneity, when by coincidence things are happening together, at the same time?

The commotion could create confusing anarchy with the inter-mingling of separate things into mere components of each other. Things are better examined if separated into isolation.

But combinations are frequent for contrast, comparison, and variety.

Multiplicity gives us more to work with.

Are you referring to co-ordinating combinations of complexity? The enlarging of the micro- into the macro-?

Complex systems lead to the brain's self-defeatingly getting out of hand. Interconnections often break open and apart. One depart-ment is an alien obstruction to another, unable to coalesce. Depart-mental red tape creates intermingling confusions of unworkable bureaucracies, compartmentally speaking.

Do things anachronistically fall apart into stray elements of frag-mentary incohesiveness, anarchy's self-ineffectual parody?

Of course. What else is new?

REMEMBER THIS MEMORY DIALOGUE, PROVIDED YOUR MEMORY DOESN'T BOG OR BLUR YOUR BRAIN IN A FOG.

How does memory differ from the event or experience that mem-ory derives from and pertains to?

The original event or experience has to come first. Memory comes later, as the derivative that mixes with other stuff in the brain, thus distorting the original event or experience, through time and imag-ination.

Thanks. I'll remember what you said.

How accurately?

Distortedly. Now it becomes mine, no longer yours.

You're a thief. You stole it.

Am I welcome to it?

Help yourself. But do me justice.

I'm not a cop, lawyer, or magistrate. I play fair. I call it like I see it,
like an umpire.
Is it foul or fair,
or strike or ball,
or what inning over-all?
Above all, what's the score,
as well as details more?
Put that in your memory bag,
so that the whole experience doesn't lag.

CONVERSATION AT FULL PACE

Life is one thing after another?

Of course. Otherwise you'll get too crowded.

So events have to be separated in order not to simultaneously happen all at once?

Yes. That's what time is for.

What is time for?

To prevent everything from happening all at once. It keeps things apart, so each event can "breathe" and be taken in for what it individually is, as an entity of happening.

Boy, are you profound!

That's what brains are for. To take each thing that goes on, and look into it.

That makes me lazy enough to get exhausted.

Yes. Monitor your energy. *Save* some energy left over for *savor*-ing things.

Boy, you're intellectually hot!

I take stimulation from being in conversation with you.

Sure, you goad me on to keep pace, and I do the same to you.

It takes two to tango and also to converse, provided vitality is mustered into a duo dynamo.

Conversation is binary.

Our music is contrapuntal.

Thanks for setting me into motion.

Likewise you too.

Well, let's slow down.

Exhaustion is one of sleep's key preliminaries.

And sleep's function is to refresh, so things can start "wheeling" again.

So *motion* is life?

But I get dizzy from all the *commotion.*

Get your balance.

But what's being balanced?

You're going too far for me to keep up with.

DIFFICULTY VERSUS EASE

What's life? And who am I? Those are leading questions for philosophy to discard as metaphysical impossibilities to get a grip on. Why bother?

Their unanswerability frustrates me intellectually. Why can't I just give up?

You like being challenged by difficulty, and blindly go to the point of no return.

Well, at least these problems are deep.

So is the sea. But that doesn't mean you should dive in.

So you're an advocate of "safety first"?

Sure. Life is too valuable to relinquish. It's your first priority of value.

Its superiority to death is overwhelming.

Poor death. It has such a low rating.

For good reason. It's an indisputable kill-joy. It deserves a poor press of public unpopularity.

Its avoidance is our wisest act.

Good. It makes wisdom sound easy.

That's wrong. Wisdom should be a hard trial, to prove its authenticity.

Why do you make things so tough?

So we can appreciate what's easy.

That's too simple. I value profundity, which requires effort.

Efforts are infamous for getting unrewarded.

That needn't deter me.

Are you a masochistic martyr to punishment, self-inflicted?

I don't like labels.

WHAT'S DEATH'S POINT?
THERE'S NOTHING THERE.

Death is a hard act to follow.

But it's no act, in the sense that it's real. But it's also no act in another sense: that there's no action. It's a mere nothing, when it comes to consciousness.

Don't put down death. It's awesome.

But there's nothing there. It's nothing.

You mean it's an anti-life?

Not even that. It's empty.

What is it empty of?

Consciousness.

You place too much emphasis on consciousness.

I do? Try it yourself.

You mean I'll experience lack?

You won't experience it. You'll have nothing to experience with.

No faculty, or agency?

No means.

That's very mean of death.

Stop making humor. It's not funny.

Who are you to judge?

I judge from life's point of view.

Then you're biased.

I'm just being anthropological, or anthrocentric.

Your humanity blinds you to death. It limits your vision.

I see your point. But I'd rather not stray.

HUMOR CONSOLES GLOOM'S DOOM.
THERE ISN'T MUCH ROOM.

Life being only one to a customer, I'm glad to add myself to the great mass of humanity, which faces similar circumstances of limitation.

We live once. That's all we get.

But it has length enough to carry us through phases of infancy, childhood, adolescence, maturity, early middle age, late middle age, and seniority.

That's quite a show, if fullness of life is maintained.

Thus we endeavor. Shouldn't we be satisfied?

No. Greed enters into it. We want life to be stretched out in health.

But decay intervenes.

Especially toward the end.

Don't remind me.

It's already happening.

Nothing succeeds life.

Death. We feel it in anticipatory dread.

Fear is death's prematurity.

The preliminary is bad enough. The feature is devastating.

It breaks my heart, as well as other parts.

We were already forewarned.

Why not forearmed?

Preparation is laughable.

Too late for humor, except for the gallows variety.

Worn-out nature is our gallows.

If effective, they slay me.

IN BASEBALL YOU ACHIEVED SUCCESS
BEFORE FAILURE MADE YOU LESS,
AND MADE FANS CURSE INSTEAD OF BLESS.

The older you get, the worse you play
the young man's game of baseball.
In fielding, you make errors,
fumble a ground ball,
and throw the ball away,
and bat the ball very weakly,
not every month but weekly,
make the ball go into a fielder's mitt,
and strike out meekly when you try to hit.
Why? Simply because you're not fit.
So simply because baseball is a young man's game,
quit before you enter the Hall of Shame.
Your speed has slowed down to a crawl,
so plead with your manager: "That's all."
Then retire and remember your record
was once proud and to be reckoned,
before you helped your team finish second.
Off the field you were then beckoned.
Farewell to the lovely game of baseball.
As a young man it had you in thrall
before your performance faced a ruinous fall.
So now we don't find you in the dugout.
After three strikes, the umpire said "out!"
You caused too many a losing bout,
and no longer hear a fan's shout.

DIALOGUE BETWEEN TWO OLD MEN

What defines life? I've been living it a long time, despite which I don't know what it is.

It is what it is, no more and no less.

That's an unsatisfactory answer.

Well, that's all you get from me. I'm no life scientist.

I just hoped you would take a guess.

I'm not an academic, but even as an amateur I'd be ashamed to merely *guess* at what such an awesome subject like life is.

We could look it up in a dictionary, an encyclopedia, a search engine, a google, a smartphone, a wikipedia.

That's an impressively modern list.

Then why am I being old?

A modern list doesn't negate being old. You can have both at the same time.

Thanks, but I fear death.

I can't help you with that. It's *your* business.

You mean you're immune?

I'm not immune, but my fear isn't operative just now.

You're lucky.

I'll die anyway. Fearlessness can't prevent it.

Nor can fear.

Death seems impervious.

Not so loud. You might wake it up.

IF ROSE WERE STILL YOUNG

If Rose were still young now, and you're your current age of ninety-six, would impotence prevent you from making physical love with her?

Realistically, of course yes. It's a sad regret, but I'd have to submit to the realism of what my current advanced age can't do.

But wouldn't you be too tired and worn out anyway?

Sure. Even Rose wouldn't blame me. She'd understand.

That's very compassionate of her. Would she feel sorry for you?

Yes, but also for herself. It's a mixed match.

Would you be jealous if Rose took up with a younger, able-bodied man?

Yes, but I wouldn't blame her.

Are young people too entitled, and too-old people too deprived?

Yes, but I'm not envious or jealous. Love is naturally between contemporaries.

Sure. It's very generational.

What a coincidence to be contemporaries at the same time!

That's most opportune. People at the right age take advantage.

So would I. How could I blame them?

You couldn't. Temptation can be very age-related.

Many youngsters find that irresistible. Think of our inflated population!

Nothing like our inflated conversation.

LET'S TREAT US TO
A TREATISE ON TIME
IF IT ARRIVES ON TIME.

All the privileges youth has, which very old age isn't permitted!

That's the nature of the game. There's no fooling around as to youth's advantages, including sex, compared with very old age's deprivations, especially sex-related.

Well, as I'm ninety-seven, I'm forced to go along with that.

I'm glad you're reconciled. What a spoiled old brat you'd be otherwise!

The best thing is to be a spoiled *young* brat.

You can't cast a blaming finger at that.

What an influence time casts over our lives!

That's true of us, and also with our wives.

Being time-related is also how life arrives
from the mother's womb if the baby thrives.

Then is time the master of us all?

Why not? Holding us in thrall.

Is death also related to time?

Of course. Otherwise very old age would be a crime
for taking up too much of our valuable time.

FUNDAMENTAL DIALOGUE
TO NOT REMAIN IN A FOG
PURSUING LIFE'S DEFINITION
IN ITS LATEST OFFICIAL EDITION

Essentially, what's Life's essence?

If it were a champagne bottle, then "effervescence."

Don't digress. I refer to Life.

If you want a condensed breakdown of Life's definition, I can't put it in a nutshell.

Then say it right out, straight.

I think it's undefinable. Life can't be put in words.

Then what else are we using?

Our dialogue is word-centric.

Verbal usage allows communication.

Dialogue uses alternate voices.

Each voice-owner makes choices.

Otherwise, it's mere noise.

Un-elaborated, it annoys.

Words are our child-like toys.

And we're children, to begin.

Doubly together, we'll win.

But what's the contest, and what's the prize?

To reverse the usual and catch surprise.

THE DISSOLVING DIALOGUE

Life is a succession of personal events happening to the same person from birth to death.

Is that life's definition? It seems colorless.

I left out all the juicy details, resorting only to a broad outline.

Well, you haven't penetrated to life's core of essence.

That's obscured by life's sheer complexity.

Then slim it down. Cut through it. Then what's left?

Nothing but life itself.

Scientifically speaking, you haven't explained anything.

I'm too busy living life to distractedly analyze it.

Isn't life mental enough to be put into words?

It is, but not to the direct heart of the subject. I'm not an academic, just an amateur around the outside.

What about an inside scoop, like a journalist would make?

Life isn't a story. It's too diversified.

No, but isn't it a narrative?

There's no time for that, within dialogue's limitations.

I reject you for a conversational partner.

Then you cancel me out? Good riddance.

Our conflict illustrates life.

Our failure is a combination, all in one package.

Then we're in harmony?

That casts too much harm on me.

WITH YOUR OWN LOVE REMAIN,
FORBIDDING SEPARATION'S PAIN.
IT'S TO YOUR MUTUAL GAIN.
IT'S ALWAYS REQUITED,
SO YOU REMAIN UNITED.
HOW CAN YOU FIGHT IT?

My love and I stand unprotected,
once death's venom is projected.
How can I defend her, and she me,
from the separation that death will cause to be?
Death will render us apart,
which inevitably will start.
It's doomed to break our collective heart.
My dear loved one
is the one I dearly love.
If we must "go," let's go together,
since neither can bear being alone.
I'd miss her. She's my every bone.
Her skin flows over me
and we're each other's flesh.
Please don't render us apart;
don't even begin to appear to start.
Keeping us together is our art.
We're artists who paint each other
invulnerable to widowhood;
and keep our vicinity in the neighborhood.
Loss of one's love can't be withstood.
It's like a tree trunk without wood.
Remaining with her is the only good.

TOO OLD, BY FAR

I wish I hadn't grown so old. But it's too late to prevent it.

You're helpless but to submit to your advanced years.

These are accompanied by increasing fears. The fears had started off abstract and remote, but gradually appear in earnest, having a dangerously realistic quality.

That sounds ominous.

That's because the sheer numerical quantity of mere years has gotten out of hand.

What's your attitude to death, as it stands today?

Fright. But I can't fight.

No. Stay healthy as possible.

You call this pile of decrepitude "healthy"? I'm ninety-five!

Death smirks all the more, eager to pounce on the prey.

I'm scared out of my "wits."

Obviously, it's giving you fits.

I'm in a too-old bracket.

What an ugly, scheming racket! What happened to your youth?

It vanished, in all truth.

Well, what's left is "old."

I'm too scared to be bold.

That's quite true, if truth be told.

All we have is rhetoric. Thus verbally I turn my trick.

TWO MEN AT NINETY-THREE

I see all these younger people having sex fun of innuendos and teasing, with gradations of flirt. Don't you feel deprived?

No, I'm too tired and worn out. At ninety-three, it's long past the time to complain.

Certainly it's not too late now, being overdue. The older we manage to get, the more ripe is complaint time of self-pitying deprivation.

That's the nature of the game: to gripe about something that's too late to fix.

Isn't that the nature of regret?

Don't fret.

But at least we don't confuse each other for someone else.

Leave others out of it. You're only you.

Stop drooling like an ancient. Where's your spark of youth?

Consumed.

That means not resumed.

We're harmless victims of future death.

Don't let that take away your scant breath.

But I'm helpless to protest.

Then you don't pass the test.

What test are we up against?

Fortitude.

Is that a real attitude?

No. We're pathetic and crude,
and barely capable of a mood.
Yet nominally we're still alive,
and cling to crumbling pride.

We make a few jokes
on the sound of rhyme
to while away our time.

It's too innocent to be a crime.

Thus we reverse being a baby
who's always forgiven, maybe.

SIMPLE BUILDING BLOCKS

Life goes from one thing to another.

Boy, are you profound! How did you figure *that* out?!

Don't be sarcastic. Simple statements can be building blocks leading to significant complexities.

Give me an example.

Give me a break. I can't think of any at the moment. I was just being offhand. I can't prove everything I say, or even justify it. I'm often casual.

Maybe you're too loose.

Like a French artist.

Who?

Too-loose Lautrec.

Stop being facetious with a nominal pun. We're dealing on serious matters.

What makes them so serious?

Me. That's how I designate them.

Are you the ruler of the world?

Literally, no. But it would be nice.

DIALOGUE OF DEATH-SUBJECTED LIFE

I'm so glad I'm alive. But Death is another story.

It's not any story. There's nothing there.

I want no part of that disgusting phenomenon.

It's not any phenomenon. There's nothing to report.

Well, Life is my turf. That's where I want to stay.

But you can't. If Death wants you to be incorporated with its "billions" of other victims over history, you're a "dead duck."

I've lived a good Life. Can't I get rewarded?

No, only *within* Life. That's where the honors come, if any. Once that session is over, you'll become nothing.

What about "heaven"?

It's bullshit.

Do I have any recourse?

Not without self-mobile organic power.

I'm growing pessimistic by the hour.
Why can't I be a simple flower,
only to wilt
by the way I'm built,
and simply die without guilt?
A plot of grass will "mourn" me.
With my petals gone, how can I "be"?

Death is Life's extraordinary fee. By the way, that flower never had consciousness. At least you did and do.

I'LL NOW RELATE
DEATH'S EMPTY STATE.
(IT'S SURE NOT GREAT.)

Death will find me unprepared
(except a will and other documents left behind)
for the "nothing" I enter forever
without a social personality
to defend my own interests
like a lawyer, so to speak.
I won't be able to negotiate with other fallen people
what it "feels like" to be dead,
comparing notes.
I'll be represented by no votes,
in this democratic non-election,
being assigned to no special section
of "Neverland,"
which is where I'll "land"
(or so I predict)
as an imaginary district,
and lose the ability to peep,
in this strict state more rigid than sleep.
Thus I'll be numb,
profoundly mentally dumb.
To tide me over, there's no crumb.

HOW TIME ACCOUNTS FOR HUMAN NATURE

Life goes from one thing to another?

Yes, successively in sequence, using all the time available for each
episode, venture, event, or happening, for as long as it takes, some-
times more than one at any given time.

138

Using up the time in each case makes the individual that much older?

Yes, sometimes unaware to him or her. The old song goes: "As time goes by."

That sounds so nostalgic.

Yes, but maybe too sentimental.

We emotional people can't help it.

It's in our nature.

Well, who's going to fight nature? Not me.

BEING INSIDE THE OUTSIDE, BEYOND THE REACH OF EGO'S PRIDE

My end of life is approaching.
Do I need any coaching
for what to do at the final moment?

No, you're momentarily at a loss.
Your last fatal moment is slipping by.
Why not have a good cry?

I tried, but my tears were dry.
Finally it struck me—I was already dead,
but the fact hadn't reached my head.

So, were you stranded on the Border?

Eternity seemed in disorder.
I peeked to see what was beyond.
But I got stuck in the Divide,
and missed the tourism of a good ride
along the edge of Death's inside.

What would you have found?

Nothing: weighing a negative pound,
airlessly hoisted above the ground.

Ground!? But I thought it would have been a cloud.

Don't blurt your ignorance all too loud.

But the Boundary is known to be unknown.

Well, people can guess, being theory-grown.

But aren't you supposed to be dead?

It slipped my mind. I slipped away,
and quietly announce my end of play.

THE CRASH AFTERMATH

If an airplane (on which you were a passenger) were plunging deep down toward a crash, what would you do?

Be scared out of my wits, if any were left.

Then what would you do?

Pragmatically survey mentally where the plane might land, and then figure out what chances if any were left for survival on the particular sea or land that receives the crash.

That's really keeping your head under the extremity of adverse circumstances.

Sure. I was desperate.

Did it really happen?

Actually, yes.

What resulted?

I'm dead.

You're a ghost?

Yes. By coincidence, just in time for Halloween.

What a lucky coincidence!

That's my celestial good luck, if any.

Well, I don't envy you. Being a ghost has no future. That's what haunts me about your predicament.

Don't get rid of me so fast.

Stop clinging. What will you wear for the Halloween party?

I'm coming as myself. What could be more authentic than that?

BEING PESSIMISTICALLY HONEST

Does that slow down the aging process?

Only by the gimmick of auto-suggestion.

But does it actually *work*, to reverse the aging process?

Of course not. Don't be stupid.

You're not a mystic?

I wouldn't be caught dead being a mystic. It's too unrealistic.

However, you *could* be caught dead by becoming too old.

I'm not a miracle worker.

Not even with your gimmick of thinking "young" thoughts?

It doesn't always, sometimes never, work.

Evidently. You look obscenely too old for words.

Well, that's the age I actually am.

At least you're being honest.

That won't help me against death's threat.

You're so realistically pessimistic!

Honestly is of little use. Death won't get fooled by it to give me a discount for honesty.

No. Honesty even *encourages* death?

Death isn't in the mind-reading or character-raising department.

THE DIALOGUE OF DECISIVE DOUBT

After life is done, is there anything else?

No. I wish there is.

What about so-called "heaven"?

It's only a myth, to delude people into stop being scared.

Then religion is phony?

It's a bunch of baloney.

What about a "savior"?

There is none. It's to give people hope that there's any more to life— which there isn't.

Why am I being deceived?

It's a class action, a mass deception. You all get cheated into a false belief.

Then religion is a crook?

They even have it in a book.

It's called a bible.

That sounds tribal.

Then you have to ignore this fake promise?

Keep persistful of your doubt, Thomas.

UNEVEN DIALOGUE

(Man speaks first.)

I love you with all my heart. Please marry me.

Why should I? I don't love you.

But if you only try to, once you marry me your love can grow by leaps and bounds. Just marry me first and see what happens.

What a rash proposal! I'm wealthy and you're poor. You love me, and I don't requite you. In point of fact, you don't even attract me.

Stop handicapping me.

I'm young and beautiful; and you're old and poor. This would-be romance stinks at the start.

It's not a very promising proposition, but couldn't you take a chance on me?

I'm eligible and you're not. It's too uneven.

True, I may not be a bargain, but can't the sincerity of my love tempt you?

On that merit, on that basis, no.

Have you turned me down?

I've made that *apparent.*

Then you're in no danger of becoming *a parent.*

On the contrary, I'm engaged to a rich stud who'll make a mother out of me with a future baby.

Then I guess I have to give up, maybe.

THE PRE-DEATH BEDSIDE VISIT

It's a fair mathematical equation that the more time goes by, one's past bloats and one's future shrinks.

Yes, finally the point is reached—

Go no further. The more life drags out, the more death draws near, with the exchange value spelling absolute terror at the perilous border.

Then with extinguished breath, your memories all disappear in instant snuffing out.

I'm reaching that point.

I'm much younger, so can you put me on your will with a generous donation to my comfort, since you'll die childless?

No, I don't like you that much.

Who'll get your saved-up bundle? Not your wife, who numbers among the recent dead.

Are you deaf? Let me repeat: I don't like you enough to put you on my will.

Am I being punished for a past offense?

Yes. You insulted me. That's a personal crime.

What was its nature?

How can you expect me to remember, me being memory-compromised?

But we became friends.

My will is finished and you're not on it.

I said something that rankled you? How about forgiving me, with a generous donation to my comfort? I'm loyal, being at your bedside.

I don't recall your offense. But let it stand as reason enough to deprive you.

Your lack of charity is appalling. I'm practically in rags. I eat lousy food.

My eyes are too dry to cry for your welfare.

You're a dying rat.

STANDING UP AND FIGHTING FOR YOUR RIGHT

Life is our greatest blessing. We're lucky to have it.

The problem is: "Here today, gone tomorrow."

Yes. Death spoils life.

But only at the end. We got a big deal *before* that.

Yeah, but the end is the killjoy. What's a worse anti-climax than that rat of a spoiler?

Yeah, Death ought to be outlawed. It's human nature's ruination.

Not just in this nation, but all over.

Is there a lawyer, who knows a lot of languages, who we can hire to represent our human right to protest Death's disgraceful interference with the right to go on living?

No. Death is a force of nature, and can't be denied.

It comes as an all-sweeping tornado, one individual at a time.

We can institute a class-action suit. There's enough of us to win out if we all pull together.

There's power in numbers.

We'll sign a petition.

What address should we send it to?

Stop with your legal technicalities.

But this is a transaction.

Big deal. Life is too wonderful to be denied.

It's the right side to be on. *(They shake hands, as a unity signal.)*

**MEMORY IS A MIXED BAG
LIKE LIFE ITSELF, WHICH IT WILL DRAG
FROM THE DEEP OR NEAR PAST,
AS LONG AS WHAT IS DREDGED WILL LAST,
DEPENDING ON HOW IT WAS CAST.**

Memory is a weird thing.
So much of the Past it will bring,
whose wealth it might restore,
but also, sadly, more.
It will re-enact heartbreaks—
scattered leaves it sometimes rakes,
that make you still have the shakes
of deep remorse or regret.
So memory is a fifty-fifty bet.
Will you greatly rejoice? Or regret?
Both. We re-mourn the good that's lost.
All memory comes with a cost.
Some nostalgia is even forced.
So when thinking back, keep fingers crossed.
Make sure when you reminisce
that you gain more than you miss.
Remember darling love's long lasting kiss?
Memory gives you some of Hell, but also bliss.
It's a gamble, maybe "hit-or-miss."
So make sure when you recall,
when thinking back, keep your eye on the ball.
Let big things enlarge, but small things shrink,
and be unfazed when your eyelids blink.
If tears start crawling, wink

and seize what remains of the link.
Memory can fool you a lot.
Sometimes it's wise to blot
the next connective dot.
Confusing what's what
can take you far back;
and then you start to lose track.
But let's all praise Memory,
which is spoiled by Death's enmity,
who never claimed to be a friend of me.

I CHANGED MY MIND.
TO OLD AGE I'LL BE KIND.

Ninety years is too long to live.
The body really has nothing left to give.
So give up right there,
to limit further years of despair.
Enough being more than enough,
then cut off your life in a snuff.
Resort to immoral suicide
to invade your mortal inside,
since that's what you currently decide.
Thus welcome to dull oblivion:
your next residence to "live" in.
Yes, but what does it win?
Not all consciousness is a sin.
No, I refuse to lose.
So I'll live on and drink booze.
Death I'll snub with polite excuse,
with dwindling faculties yet to use.
When Death wants me, he'll choose.

SYMPTOMS OF DECAY,
TO YOUR INCREASING DISMAY

You're losing your power, getting weaker.
Thus my outlook is bleaker.
Old age is losing the fight
to imitate youth's might.
What youth did casually,
old age is a casualty
of its hanging on too long
till your co-ordination is wrong
between competing faculties.
Keeping together is a prolonged tease.
You're beginning to fall apart.
Making excuses is your fine art.
Society needs apologizing to
for all the things you're unable to do,
which youth did in a cinch.
You're losing what you had, inch by inch.
Your flesh is too sagging to resist a pinch.
Thus wrap it up and say goodbye.
Take a good look: you'll miss the eternal sky
that whirled about overhead.
Your sight falters. You're almost dead.

HOW TO ELIMINATE DEATH
(BUT DON'T HOLD YOUR COLLECTIVE BREATH)

Why does death always have to spoil life?

It doesn't right away. Only at the end.

Even *then*, why does death appear,
with its morbid lack of cheer,
when life has proven so very dear?

In order not to make earth so jammed up
with all generations of population.
There'll be a shortage of enough room
for everybody to breathe at the same time,
both exhale and inhale in unison.

Then evolution should make humans thinner,
for the whole human race to become a winner.
We just shouldn't eat too much dinner.

But courting malnutrition is to be a sinner.
We need nourishment to preserve the inner.

SUMMING UP LIFE IN AN AMBITIOUS TOME MULTI-COLORED, BUT ALSO MONOCHROME

What's the essence of Life,
condensed in a proverbial nutshell?
It's too complex to be summing up.
It overflows itself,
rather than being a trophy on the shelf.
How lucky that it takes a long time
to complete its lengthy prose and pithy rhyme!
We have infancy, youth, and middle age,
till we sprawl across the last page.
Now the book is closed.
What a lot there, enclosed!
History has too much brisk research to do,
to get the lowdown on me and you.
Will it reveal a scandal? Yes, a few.
But while you're writing your review,
don't forget to live and laugh
before you finish your first draft.
But if you reach an impasse,
take a break and polish your craft.

Be verbally precise, if you're not daft.
If you're stuck somehow, do your math
to prove you're not on the wrong path
and acquire the publisher's wrath.

A RELUCTANT GOODBYE.
ONLY YOUR MOURNERS WILL CRY?

Getting old is too precarious.

Oh, your life was so various!
It's a precious cargo
that once had far to go.
Now it's seeing the target:
which is to be able to forget.
Relinquish everything you could possibly get.
All your memories will die out,
even of former loves.
Flesh will decide how long you'll keep them
before they abandon you and you weep them.
Can you hold on for dear life?

No. It's ebbing out
and resisting my feeble shout.
Anyway, what was it all about?

You loved this woman with all your heart.
How automatically you have to part!
Your weakening flesh
can't keep the spark afresh.
Her image appears in your head
which becomes a skull, so you're dead,
and where is she?

Out somewhere, maybe floating free.

THE VACCINATION ERA.
IS NOTHING ANY CLEARER?
I'M A PANDEMIC BABY
WHOSE LUCK HAS CHANGED TO MAYBE.

(1)

Fear spreads its disease
in deathly horror,
specializing on the elderly,
none of whom is a celebrity.

(2)

Everyone's death status is weighing
on longevity's balance,
so prayers are secretly spreading
to private gods wherever.
"Keep alive" is the goal
in all the medical cases.
"How longer do I have?" everyone's wondering.
All the fears have a common object.
Survival's obsession is society's craze.
In this whole social arena
comes the menacing death subpoena
served without notice.
How will the gods of death vote us?
Each individual at a time
commits the vulnerability crime.
Am I the appointed victim?
I've got to work the health system.
I can't resort to mysticism.
I'm split into what schism?
The worry bug has got me.
Maybe death forgot me?
I depend on luck,

so I have to work up my pluck.
Maybe everybody wear a mask,
so I don't even have to ask.

SAD PREDICAMENT

My life is declining to lonely nostalgia for increasingly lost youth.

You're paying too high a price for surviving your old friends.

Why did they have to die or relocate?

Nostalgia can eat you up, crumble you up, throw you away.

Feeling sorry for myself is a sad way to waste my last years.

Is there any remedy?

Reading doesn't work for me any more, whether fiction or non-fiction. They all bore me. Same with television and radio.

Well, at least you could eat.

There's too much empty time between meals.

Fill up the time when not your stomach.

When I *do* eat, I put too much emphasis on what I so hastily devour. Then I have to wait too long for the next meal, and meanwhile lose my appetite into the bargain.

You have lots to moan about.

Moaning is lonely. Groaning is at least more social when I get someone to groan to, in full English.

Get out more and meet new people, if not neighbors you habitually ignore.

As you can readily see, I'm too wheelchair bound and chronic illness ridden, confined to indoors.

Will you kill yourself?

Are you crazy!? I love life!

NOT GETTING SUED FOR PLAGIARISM, BUT BY WHOM?

Can you sum up your philosophy of life?

No. Life is too mercurial and improvisational to be statically summed up into a tiny nutshell. Life has a broadening sweep, and can't be tamed to a one-sentence definition.

Are you implying that life is too restless to pose for you, as opposed to the way a life model can be still enough to pose for a class of art students?

Precisely. You tore the words right out of my brain.

But that's plagiarism.

Not until you write down my ideas for me to have then read, after your getting published to be plagiarized from.

Good. That cuts off loopholes for you, so I won't have to counter-sue you.

Thanks for the good will.

I beg to remain on congenial terms. Original ideas shouldn't divide us, when one of us is so mere a copycat as to plagiarize the truly authentically original other.

For whose benefit should I agree with you?

The main thing is to prevent the culprit from committing unfairness.

Shouldn't that go without saying?

Maybe we should both agree to share the same loopholes.

Who's the one accused?

The same one to be excused.

I'm not sure of my role.

That's easy. I'm the opposite pole.

Let's get this competition under control.

Are there any ground rules?

That would eliminate the fools.

YOU'RE PRACTICALLY FACING IT.

You're in the helpless part of old age, where you're getting more and more doddering.

I'm barely hanging on.

Is death pre-savoring you?

He's eyeing me with rabid appetite, virtually slavoring.

Are you on your way out?

Death is champing at the bit.

You have that hangdog look like a ripe victim of juicy saliva.

If there's nothing after death, I unwillingly submit.

Don't disappoint death by not co-operating.

Death is not a person. Why do I personify him like a human killer?

Why deny yourself the consolations of metaphoric imagination, at this perilous moment?

This is a word barrier, to beguile the time before my body gives in.

WHAT IS THE PAST?

Sex and romance are so far behind me, that youth seems like a phantasmagoria enigma I never had.

Yet it features prominently in your memory.

Memory feels like collecting stamps or signatures or clippings in a scrapbook, nothing to do with the people remembered.

At other times, their images are the real deal.

How my attitudes to the past vary!

Sure. We have a versatile repertoire of past scraps filtered along meanderingly.

The past is phony pretense that you're reliving it.

Well, it's a reasonable facsimile.

But it's phony.

I accept being fooled by the illusion.

Is the past real?

No. Maybe it's a false construct, fodder to our imagination, like a punch-and-judy show, or baby dolls clutched or hugged by little tots in the innocent act of falling away asleep.

Go ahead, dream away. Pretend you're young. Will that bring you there?

No, but shouldn't the brain be working as a memory function?

The past is impossible to drag back, being too distinctive.

But approximation is a real personal industry.

PUTTING LIGHT ON BEING DOOMED

Death is a void. But can I avoid it?

Only while you keep up your old age medical care and safety. But too much old age has a limit, and that's where death comes in.

I don't appreciate that old age appreciates so, adding up to the point of no return.

You just overdo what's fatal to overdo: namely, old age's increasing bodily deterioration where finally there's a "critical mass" that does you in.

In other words, I lived too long?

That's putting it simply.

In the long run, living wears out.

Don't remind me. Putting off death as long as possible is my daily selfish concern of self-preservation.

Well, life is worth holding on to, even when you've outlived youth.

Ideally, youth should go on forever.

Ideals challenge reality, but guess who wins?

Reality is death's assistant?

These fancy terminologies just slay me.

Aren't we "too clever by half"?

"Whistling in the dark" is our desperate maneuver. It won't work.

Not for a while. We depend on the temporary kindness of word barriers.

Like "the handwriting is on the wall."

These words fail before death's wordlessness.

What about "Death has the last laugh"?

That's not, nor ever was, funny.

THE MEANINGS OF WORDS

Some memories, stay away from: filled with regret, remorse, indignities, heartbreaks, painful nostalgia.

I already do what you say. I monitor my memories to limit them to the comfort side.

I avoid the tiny deaths of pain, like I'll try putting off the major

Death himself if I see him stalking me against the safeguards of safety and accident prevention.

Why is pain so painful?

Because that's why we use the word "pain." We want to honor the accuracies of our word usages and designations. I honor the dictionary definitions of our words.

That's a tribute to language itself.

Yes, language helps to put things where they belong in the compartments of our housekeeping.

Should I buy an apron to look the role?

Appearances aren't always necessary to keep up.

Good. But for social approval I'll keep shaving.

If I live in the social world, I want to act the role.

That's why we have habits.

But I don't want the bad habit of addiction.

You've already added "bad" and "good" to your life's vocabulary.

Whatever comes in handy is good.

Sure. That's where "opportunity" comes in.

Life is mainly practical.

That's more helpful than being theoretical.

I think your theory is correct.

A BRIEF VERBAL SCRIMMAGE,
GIVING AN UNPLEASANT IMAGE

Instead of saying that someone's dead, could you just call him "a spent force"?

Sure, but it amounts to the same thing, as a kind of euphemism. What's your point?

"Being dead" is a commonplace word usage. Being "a spent force" is a less common usage.

Boy, are you profound, when it comes to words!

You were being ironical, at my expense.

Sorry if I seemed to be making fun of you. That was impolite.

Thanks for apologizing. I excuse you.

Thanks for being so patronizing.

I didn't intend to be.

It sounded like it.

It was in my tone?

That's what I detected.

Maybe you're paranoid.

If so, then it becomes my fault?

That's the way I engineered it to be. I always like to come out on top, morally speaking.

Thanks for your confession. Hypocrisy is your profession.

THE BEFORE-AND-AFTER SEQUENCE OF MENTAL TRANSFERENCE WITHIN THE "SPACE" OF TIME

Is it possible to have a memory of what you didn't previously experience?

No. Memory is a copy-cat. You can't invent it out of whole cloth. It has to be a brainy aftermath of what you personally went through, a sort of replica.

Otherwise you're inventing it?

Yes. It's a lie unless it reflects on the previous raw material of personal experience.

Memory is a secondary derivative of an already experienced event?

Yes, even if you misinterpret that previous event.

So memory can go out of joint with what it refers to?

Yes. It could sully that experience with distortion and inaccuracy.

That betrays your integrity?

You can call it that, in a quirk of speech.

But some memories are lucidly faithful to what they're based on.

That's an immaculate conveyance of the sacred source, intactly confirmed after the event itself that was pure prototype of the first order.

The sequence of before and after is the lesson you've drilled upon me.

You got it.

It's indelible. The fish of raw experience is hauled out of the ocean of memory.

Not without a few fishy splashes.

That's why the fisherman has a wide-brimmed hat.

HOW I LULL DEATH TO DELAY.
I BEGUILE HIM AS AN EASY PREY,
SO HE GIVES ME ANOTHER DAY.

Old age has driven me up to the edge of Death,
so I mourn myself and cry.
I don't even have the energy to die,
but instead become inorganic.
I'm too unemotional for panic,
so become as dull as a stone
that lies in the gutter all alone
in its dead weight defying gravity.
I'm too innocent for depravity.
I belong to the mineral species,
and immovably do what's easiest,
which is to be thoughtless for a while,
breathing at the lowest ebb
like a barely dead spider in its web.
If this goes on any longer,
I'm unlikely to get much stronger.
Death is too lazy to bother me,
hypnotized by my state of being.
How proud I am to influence Death
not to provoke me further
in administering his usual murder.
Instead, he's so placid and calm.
My purpose is to obviously disarm,
so I weakly exert my remaining charm,
and make an elaborate decoy
to put Death off from his object to destroy.

HARD TO FOOL DEATH
AND RETURN WITH YOUR WHOLE BREATH.

The way not to die
is to seem to comply
to Death's instruction, but to lie.

Fooling him is hardly a cinch.
He won't give you an inch
in your mortal tussle.
He even makes the leaves rustle
on any ordinary tree.

But what will he make of extraordinary me?
I'll give him such resistance
as to increase his insistence.
But I need good luck's persistence.

What form will that take?

I'll have to think that over.
I'll let you know what I discover.

Good. I'll be all ears.

But you may have to wait.
Death may not fall for my bait.
He has its own design,
so radically different from mine.

Then I'll give up right here,
since the prospect omits cheer.
It's quite predictable
that he'll adhere to the same principle:
namely, he'll turn up invincible.

TRYING TO FOOL DEATH
PANTINGLY DRAINS YOUR BREATH.

Death is hardly easy to cheat.
I offer him bread and say, "It's whole wheat."
But he'll say "I want whole grain.
Now I'll enter you with extra pain
for trying to fool me.
Trifling with me at your expense
requests the penalty I dispense
to you for being a wise guy.
If you resist, I'll make you cry
in such a way that the tears will flow
to your whole tomb below.
All your mourners will get the drizzle,
as your bones rot with extra fizzle
like a big town under a missile."
That was the end of me.
I lit up like a Christmas tree
and smiled my adieu to Life,
but all the lights blanked out,
doffed by Death to dim any doubt.
My loss was a one-sided rout,
with no signs of a return bout.

OLD MAN BEING INTERVIEWED

You're so old now. Looking back, did you get enough fun out of life?

Compared to other men who've lasted as long as me, it's hard to tell.

You can interview them.

At this age, their brains aren't reliable enough.

Is yours?

Yeah. I'm well preserved, comparatively.

Then you've done well for yourself, all told.

I'm not boasting about it. Life is a good bargain, but the deal is disappointing when you throw Death into the reckoning.

Yeah. Death is a killjoy.

It makes life seem too temporary, too "borrowed."

Oh, don't be spoiled. Life is still the best deal you can get, in this open market.

Yeah, but not in the end, where "the Spoiler" lurks.

Are you death-obsessed?

Yeah. It pours rain over Life's planned picnic.

But the picnic had time to take place before the rains weighed in.

Youth was terrific, especially the sex part. But old age is the killer.

Does that make Life a bad bargain?

Not altogether bad; but limited.

TWO OLD MEN AND SEX

I'm too old for sex.

So be it. Did you have enough sex before your old age disability?

No. So how can I make up for it?

It's too late now.

But that's tragic. Couldn't I revive my last phase of youth?

No. You're too late. It's your penalty for not harboring all your youthful chances earlier.

Well, I'll take consolation in other ways.

Like what?

Like meditating and contemplating philosophically.

In what categories?

Metaphysically, ethically, judicially, aesthetically, scientifically, astrologically, historically, nature studies, etcetera.

That covers a wide berth of territories.

I'm not daunted. It's all in the mind.

The mind is so tiny to accommodate so much.

It sure does go a long way.

But it can't compensate for my loss of youth and therefore the sex I didn't get enough of.

Be philosophical about it.

I'll sure get enough Death.

That's where time is so generous.

TWO OLD MEN CONVERSE.

What am I doing alive, when my two best friends are dead?

You're just luckier then they were and are.

But how can I be luckier, when I miss them so much?

You can still manage to live without them. But *they* have no choice in the matter.

So should I bear up without them, and enjoy life anyway?

That's your only alternative. Go on missing them grievously, but be thankful that you're alive enough to do so and be able to carry on without them.

But my nostalgia is aching horribly. I'm plagued with my loving memories of them.

Don't ask me for empathy and pity. Enjoy your survival of them to whatever reluctant degree you possibly can.

But then I feel hard-heartedly disloyal to both, riddled with guilt.

No sympathy from me. You're selfishly better off than they are, right now.

You're asking me to be reconciled?

I'm not asking. I'm advising.

Am I too sentimental?

Your sentimentality is dripping all over you like Summer's heat and humidity of over a hundred degrees.

That's too much to bear.

Just sweat it out. Have a stiff lip with stoical fortitude. Buy a fan.

You're my fan. I'll do as you say.

What's my reward?

I'll now appoint you my third best friend, despite your "still-living" classification.

I hope it doesn't put me in the "doomed" category.

WHO'S HURRYING
WITH WHAT WORRYING?

Death caught me unprepared,
only half dressed
with one shoe on and one shoe off.
But I had to go when commanded,
independently of where I'd landed,
which was right at Life's border,
despite my apparent disorder

of clothes all in a heap.
My mourners prepared to weep.
Death made a clean sweep
and cleared up all the remains,
and the Funeral Director was at pains
to catch his due date
for my corpse to meet its fate,
and not a minute too late.
So we were all in a hurry.
What was this unseemly worry?
But Eternity was slow to respond.
It would never be prematurely conned,
living vastly in the Beyond.

WHAT HAPPENED TO SIMPLE WALKING?
(OLD AGE DIALOGUE EXCHANGE)

As I go on aging, I cover less and less territory on my own two feet. I used to walk East Side, West Side, all around the town. Now I'm limited to shorter and shorter distances, till at this rate my cherished mobility becomes grounded like a paralytic.

I'm in the same boat. The nostalgia becomes helplessly passive on my own two feet. I can't go anywhere at will! I'm the captive of my own immobility, like being in jail with close four walls.

The nostalgia then becomes more acute, since you're unable to satisfy its normal yearnings of fulfilling the covering of the given territories.

I'm losing easy habits that used to be automatic and were assumed to be taken for granted.

Old age kills you in small increments that eventually add up to personal catastrophe. Being stuck and dependent on help has come into nightmare reality.

When the nightmare becomes daily, you simply adjust.

Yes, with constant memory reminders of how superior the past was, in youth's entitled insolence.

Automatic assurance in the kingdom of privilege has become a doomed dream.

GOING OUT WITH A LAUGH?
IT'S NOT ON DEATH'S NORMAL GRAPH.

Death and I got into a screaming fit.
I begged him to allow me to die with wit,
but he insisted on an orderly procedure
leading me to my fatal seizure.
Death pompously insisted on dignity
in his ceremoniously ousting me from life.
I wished to defy tradition
and die jokingly on my outward mission.
He accused me of being too unorthodox
by squeezing myself into the coffin's box
with my corpse sporting a smile
on my withered skull as I end my trial
just in time for Halloween's play
where I'll be the featured guest.
The director will honor my request
to be irrelevantly hilarious
by spouting jokes unseriously various.

THE TIRELESS GOURMAND

I feel like a waiter in a restaurant.

Of all reasons, why? Aren't you old enough to be long retired?

I'm waiting on my customer, who's Death, and I'm the meal he's going to devour.

Will he tip you afterwards?

Maybe, but not too generously. His tireless appetite awaits other waiters.

As a gourmet?

No, as a gourmand.

Does he regurgitate every meal, in order to keep his appetite fresh and empty for accommodating later waiters?

Yes. What a constant round of pleasures for him daily and nightly!

His eating may be pleasurable, but his post-meal regurgitating may be momentarily painful.

It keeps him feeling unentitled.

What a phony! I envy his life. He's a spoiled brat.

I must stop acting like a reluctant feast, with all the trimmings. I could just hear his voracious salivating.

ANYTHING BEATS DEATH.

Your life has been an agony of suffering and misery. Finally you're old enough to die. After what you've been through, don't you welcome Death as a great relief?

No. I still preferred my horrible life to Death's grim prospect.

Then you're a masochist?

Anything beats Death.

Well, you're certainly illustrating that precept.

Thanks. I defend my past horrors from Death's endless nothingness.

Is "all well that ends well"?

Sure. If Shakespeare said that, who am I to contradict that wise guy?

You sure got a powerful pre-endorsement to back your theory up.

Well, time for me to die now.

It will banish your awful memories, thanks to your nemesis, Death.

TWO OLD MEN IN THE SAME BOAT, SO TO SPEAK

I'm getting so much older that I'm scared of death.

Me too, for that matter.

We're both in the same boat?

Yeah, so we can be fellow sympathizers.

Well, we know how each other feels.

Can we give each other therapy?

Yeah, we'll take turns. But that's difficult, since we're both patients.

Can you be both a therapist and a patient at the same time?

Yes, we're both under the same shadow.

You mean both under the same cloud.

But we're indoors, so there's no cloud to be under.

Don't cloud the issue.

Anyway, how could we cure each other?

Through mutual sympathy?

Sympathy is not therapy. It's like looking in a mirror.

Maybe the mirror is cracked.

Then it gives a crooked reflection.

Maybe not crooked, but flawed.

Let's not split hairs.

Hairs are too skinny to split.

I'm bald anyway.

For that matter, so am I.

My baldness reflects the mirror.

No, the mirror is sharper.

That's a cutting remark.

AN OLD MAN'S MEMORIES SHOULDN'T BE HIS ENEMIES.

The older I get,
the more I forget,
much to my regret.
The memories I cherish
first seemed to perish.
I recover and put them back on
to newly dwell upon,
reassured they're not gone.
The ones I recovered
are the most beloved.
The memories I aim for
are what I'm given no blame for,
and am easily forgiven,
happily recalled to live in.
May no forgetful oblivion
wash away my wife, Vivian.

MORE GOODBYES
WITH SYMBOLICALLY WET EYES
FOR THOSE OLD GIRLS AND GUYS

So many former friends who died!
Yet with them I feel still allied
in memory's spirit
of willed recollection,
to dip into my collection
and find them there in full body
and identifiable face
to somehow keep apace.
In memory still being together
allows me to weather
time's awful passage
that falls out of fashion.
I'm still full of passion
for those unreturning friends
and their unassuming ends.
We never made proper amends.

TIME'S FREE DEFINITION

What's time, anyway?

It's what prevents everything from happening at once.

You mean it prevents simultaneous coinciding?

Yes.

Elucidate.

Different events happen: separated by time, which provides breathing space between those occurrences, so they can be singled out and analyzed, and made into order.

You mean sequence?

And significance of values and consequences.

You don't say!

Yes, I do say.

Well, you're a smart fellow, to think these things up.

But it's real.

All right, if you insist.

Yes I do.

All right. I'll buy it.

It's free.

DIALOGUE IN, AT BOTTOM, A LEAKING BOAT

If you're sailing in a boat that you notice has a leak, are you armed with swimming ability and a handy lifebuoy?

Sure. Death by water is as nasty as one of the dry occasions. The main thing is to act quick, since emergency responds to the alarm of haste, which by itself may come to waste. If you dawdle, you're doomed.

You've got to take the situation in hand, and act accordingly.

Total concentration on the relative issue may breathlessly come to the rescue.

You can't pause to think of philosophical differences between, for example, Kant and Schopenhauer, or between Kirkegaard and Thomas Dewey, and discuss such irrelevant matters at length.

No. Such considerations ignore the pragmatic urgency now so evidently at hand. The priority of "safety first" is "the elephant in the room," so to speak.

Fancy phrases won't save your life. Swift and firm action take obviousprecedence over the inappropriateness of delay, which comes potentially at a mortal cost.

It's imperative . . .

Too late!

FAILURE AT BASEBALL'S GAME
QUALIFIES ME FOR THE HALL OF SHAME.

The ball comes at me with excessive speed
to knock my glove off. It's agreed
that my days on the team are numbered
because my reflexes have slumbered
with the inability to catch or throw.
And when I bat, I swing below
or above that elusive ball,
so I needn't wait for the umpire's call.
All I hit is a bunch of air,
so fans conclude I'm not Babe Ruth's heir.
They boo instead of merely sit and stare.
My autographs are thrown out of windows
to far distances according to how the wind blows.

TO JIMMY STAGNO,
FORMER PROFESSIONAL BALLPLAYER

I meet Jimmy's car at the appointed time
outside our normal train station,
barely concealing my elation.
He drives to his local Senior Center,
where you must be public citizens when you enter.
Here in the morning we play pool

173

specialized by his creative rule.
After exchanging victories and defeats,
we repair to our usual restaurant
endowed to be inexpensive.
We discuss our beloved New York Yankees.
On our way back to the train station,
my heart bubbles up with elation
as I reminisce our relation.
We've known each other since early adolescence,
illustrating friendship's lifelong essence,
whose charm is regularity of presence,
whose enough appointments
keep long and short our disappointments.
He died at eighty eight years,
realizing our well-conditioned fears,
but makes memory appearances
to reap in my endearances.
His injury-shortened baseball career
gave him a burst of momentary cheer.
Now our proximities are approximately near.

DEFINITION OBSTINANCE

Life is what we're living. But what is it?

That's too self-explanatory for me to dignify with an answer.

Don't be a snob. Condescend to give it a try.

You mean its definition?

That's what I'm asking.

I don't know if I can oblige you.

Why?

Life is too complex. I'm no scientist or psychologist. I'm just an ordinary man trying to get through life. *Living* it is enough. Isn't it enough for you?

No. What is it?

Go consult the dictionary.

Its definition would be too short to satisfy me.

But the dictionary is a heavy book.

That doesn't carry much weight with me.

It's heavy enough to block a door with a furious storm trying to rush in through the ajar (slightly open) bottom.

Don't get melodramatic. Are you a weather man?

No, I'm a carpenter.

THE DIALOGUE THAT GOT IRRITATINGLY OUT OF HAND

In order to operate, my memory needs previous events and experiences to precede it.

That's so obvious, why are you even bothering to say it?

Because sometimes the obvious needs bothering about.

When?

Oh, don't make me have to explain things, like an unruly, pestering child.

Do I ask inconvenient questions?

You sure do.

Aren't you being discourteous instead of obliging?

Deliberately so. You make me go too much out of my way. Stop tampering with me. I'm not a gadget or service that you can conveniently turn on or off, at the whim of your service—or rather *my* service.

Stop guarding your privacy.

Stop invading me and presuming on me.

Your company is obnoxious.

Likewise yours is to me.

Let's part.

You've finally come up with a welcome note.

Good. Now we're friends again.

Not *again*. That's too presumptuous.

Have it *your* way.

HOW I LOST TOO MUCH PAST.
MEMORY WOULDN'T LET ITS RICH BULK LAST.
SO MANY EVENTS SLIPPED AWAY,
THEIR LIGHT DIMINISHED FROM THE SIGHT OF DAY.

I put my past in my memory's care,
but my memory let it drop.
It plunged to the floor with a plop.
So now my past has empty holes
and unseemly wide gaps.
Memory didn't do its duty,
so I lost too much sacred beauty
of thousands of lovely events
that wanted to return, but memory prevents,
in its dereliction of guardianship,
so I've drowned before abandoning ship.
Thus I've lost too much treasure
whose value goes beyond measure.
What happened "when" and "there"?

I looked again, but the record's bare.
Memory betrayed its sacred duty
to preserve intact all that beauty.
The past that once belonged to me
has been allowed to let its wealth go free.
Thus my past has been cut short
by the bitter knife that carved abort,
neglecting to hold the bulging fort.
I'm not normally the forgetting sort.

MORBID DIALOGUE
FORBIDDEN ON ANY CATALOG

When I go down the slippery slope,
I start to abandon hope.
Then when I reach the bottom,
Death gloats: "I've got 'em!"
I told Death: "I did the work myself,
becoming a trophy on my lifeless shelf."
Death said, "I'll take the credit,
since I grandly did the official edit."

LOOK WHO I'M JOINING!
PARDON ME FOR POINTING.
(HIS MEMORY I'M ANOINTING.)

I have only a little bit of time left
before I drag my formerly gargantuan heft
diminished into the grave,
bearing a long life that I couldn't save.
Thus I'm dead and done,
and no longer can read John Donne,

that fine metaphysical poet
who when he philosophized, was able to show it.
Thus I join him in being dead,
a disease that happened to go to my head
that was proudly able to read
John Donne and his fellow breed.
I wish to join them, I plead.

THE BANKER'S REPORT DOESN'T DISTORT. SO YOU CAN'T HOLD THE FORT IN ANY LEGAL COURT.

(1)

Life was wonderful while it lasted,
except during its sour moments.
Then like dynamite it blasted
you apart with no unity.
You can't escape with impunity.
Having lost your organic whole,
there's no brain left to console.
Anatomically you're skull and bones,
and now you can forget all your loans.
You're disallowed ever to borrow
on finance's promise of tomorrow.
You've come up empty at the end,
with no bank ever willing to lend
you enough money to recover yourself.
Old documents grow dusty on the shelf.
So at least you had a decent career
till galloping Death caught up with its fear.
What was far away is now too near.

(2)

What assets remain in your account?
Only liabilities, and to what amount?
Thus your debts are bound to outshine
all the credits that you can call "mine."
Sober yourself with a little wine.

MY WIFE AND I HAVE A BOND
THAT PIERCES US BOTH BEYOND.

I got accustomed to my wife,
but lost her along with my life.
Being alive made me deserve her,
but death is no condition to serve her.
As lovers, do we share our deaths?
No, that's too much loss of breaths.
Let's depart one at a time,
so one can mourn the other.
To die both at once is a smother.
So we'll be glad to take turns.
Let one freeze while the other burns.
So goodbye, my darling wife.
Hereby we drop our burden of strife.
Yet love pierced the animosity,
and only briefly was a casualty
on the brutal basis of reciprocity.
That's how precious you were to me.
One has gone. The other is never free
of little reminders here and there
of what my wife and I had to share.
We embraced in all our impressions
and became each other's obsessions.
My darling wife, why must you depart?

Our end is doomed to remind us of our start.
Even if we have to transcend death,
we'll back and forth produce a married breath.

REFUSAL OF PITY AND EMPATHY

Life is only one to a customer, so enjoy it while you can.

How can I? I'm in a terminal condition of extreme disease-ridden old age dragged out into feeble agony.

That's tragic. I pity you.

What can your pity do for me?

Give you empathy.

But that can't relieve my disease-ridden extreme old age on death's front doorstep dragged out into feeble agony.

Then I'm sorry you can't take my offer.

It's of no pragmatic value.

You're too opportunistic.

You're too practical-minded.

This conversation is useless. Can I offer sympathy and condolences?

Stop pressuring me. I'm vulnerable enough, already.

I LOOK ANXIOUSLY.
DOES SHE BREATHE TRANQUILLY?

I don't want her to die in her sleep,
over which I would weep.
So I gaze fiercely at her face

whose eyes are closed with an aspect of grace,
being so suspiciously still—
she could even impersonate someone ill.
Her face bears no telling clue
of perhaps a dreamlike inner view.
It's motionless—what does that reveal?
Now to take a closer look I steal,
and follow a rhythm of her breath
that happily shows no indication of death,
not even the state of her sweet soul
converging from its parts to shine as a whole.
Her eyelids quiver silently somewhat.
Oh, what a lovely wife have I got!
Thus, in the throes of relief,
I sigh and exult a thankful belief
infinitely superior to the horror of grief.

NOT GETTING WHAT YOU WANT

Once already dead, can we make a comeback?

No. Death is a finality, from which there's no recovering.

Why does it have to be that way?

It's the way Nature operates, in the biology universe, with molecules and sub-atomic particles. It's too elementary to argue against.

But people *like* Life. So why can't they hang on to it?

They have no choice. It's the way things are.

But that sounds perverse. It's not logical.

Nature has its own way.

But Nature is *me*, too.

It's *bigger* than you.

Might makes right?

Vastness is larger than the sum of its parts.

You make me feel minute.

I will be too.

When?

In a minute.

DIALOGUE OF WHAT'S FIRST, AND THEN WHAT

The memory image comes *after* the event or experience took place.

That's obvious. *Of course* an image pictorially repeats what originally happened to you in the first place. You had to *be* there first. Later, memory gets tuned in with repetitive obedience.

I'm so glad we got it straight. Sequence is important.

Can you give an example of sequence?

Sure. Tree leaves first take new Autumn colors *before* decay makes them fall to the ground, already colored.

Well done. Another example is *first* there's sex; *then* a baby comes.

Well done. Another example is: *first* a war is declared, and *afterwards* the armistice is celebrated.

Another example is *first* you weightlift, and *then* your body got strengthened.

Another example is *first* you live, and *then* you die.

Is causality the same as sequence?

Yes, but put them in the right order.

I sure will. Otherwise our point is lost.

What must precede, and what must follow, are essential examples of orderly causality and the proper successiveness of sequence within the *time* format.

Yes. I'm glad you factored *time* in.

Of course. That's how thorough I am.

Well done. Your brilliance mirrors mine.

That's funny: I thought the opposite.

MEMORY EMPTIED OUT
AFTER DEATH WON LIFE'S BOUT.

Memory helps us visit the past.
But how long will memory last?
If I'm dead, my past is gone.
What special memory will it rest upon?
Perhaps it was when I kissed Irene.
After sex with her, all was serene.
In no sense was it considered obscene.
Memories reinforced the ego.
When death kills memory, where do we go?
Into only nothing, where we can't feel woe,
or anything else, for that matter.
Before death did me, I was earth's squatter.
Now, generations have passed,
and I continue not to last.

THEN INTO NOW

As a growing up boy, I assumed "everyone else will die, but not me." Death would be for grown-ups, called adults.

I felt the same way. I felt protected by being a kid. The pink rubber ball we threw, and hit with a broomstick, was round and infinite, and lasts forever unless we hit it down a sewer.

Well, look at us now. Too slow and rickety to play, we're actually the very grown-ups who would die instead of us.

Am I the same person I used to be?

Your name hasn't changed. But your mother and father are dead.

But I'm still me.

Sure. But are you different!

So are you. But we're lifelong friends.

One of us has to "go."

Go where?

Stop being academic and pedantic.

We never used those words then.

Does the world change more than us?

The world and we grew up side by side, at the same time.

What will happen with the world? Will it die like us?

No. The little kids will take over.

That used to be us.

Well, to some extent.

SCARED OF DYING

Are you reaching the danger point of getting too old? I am, and it's starting to scare me.

Me too, I'm in the same boat. We can't keep accumulating years while continuing to get away with it. There's got to be a breaking point.

Maybe it's already too late. What's your health lately?

Wearing down.

I'm in a similar boat.

That boat seems to have a widening leak at the bottom.

I'm starting to panic. Are you?

Frankly, I'm scared stiff.

We'll remain stiff by becoming corpses.

Is it too late to resort to Religion, as a cure for our panic?

You mean Eternal Life? Heaven?

Yes. Is it possible?

Sorry, you're out of luck. Religion is a false hope.

You mean our so-called Souls can't find Eternal Life in Heaven?

It's a total illusion.

Then we have to give up?

Yes. Give up the ghost.

Who should we give it to? Who would want a stale ghost discarded by someone else? A second-hand one?

No one. Only one's own ghost would do.

For what?

For accumulating nostalgia for the old days of lost youth.

That's a beautiful dream.

Don't wake me.

RECALLING JIMMY STAGNO.
WHY ON EARTH DID HE HAVE TO GO?

Jimmy and I played ball,
no one else, with rules installed.
A broomstick and a rubber ball
were our instruments at play,
plus walls to estimate distances
and chalk to mark up the walls.
We combined our young persistences
in the big barren schoolyard.
When the rain developed, we had to quit,
consoling ourselves by practicing wit.
His jokes were cruder than mine,
but to me, they were the very sublime.
Our friendship was only at a young phase,
but blessed to enjoy many more days:
up to the very end of life for him.
But I'm surviving longevity with a big grin
to think how lucky I am
to weep with reminiscences over him.
We're half of what we used to be.
He's stuck and trapped, but I'm free
to live a little more this great life
enhanced by friendship with Jimmy.
We continue our dialogues, and I take his part
in the equal status of both being so smart
as to choose each other in our duel of art
that was even given to the occasional prank,
engaging in strong rivalry of whom to thank
the most, and in what rank.
He was short and stout, and I was tall and lank.
As the best of pals, we now say goodbye
and give me allowance to take a cry

with tears of such weeping
as to rest him secure in my keeping.

TEARS POURING FROM EYES?
YOU'RE ONE OF THOSE ABANDONED GUYS.

Death destroys relationships,
especially among the married.
One is left alive,
while the other will no longer strive,
losing the whole force of her breath
from her barren lungs
in the arena of the living.
Life is between giving
and receiving, in harness.
They need each other, honest!
But the relationship is torn apart,
when one from life has to depart
while the other lingers on,
bereaved, having lost his valued partner
into the darkness of doom,
who used to hug in the same room
as joyous bride and groom.
Thus, when time too much goes by,
the survivor has to cry
after the farewell goodbye.
Don't spare the funeral expense.
Throw in the dollars with the cents.
Nothing anymore makes sense
financially or otherwise,
when you're one of the abandoned guys
with tears dropping from your drowning eyes,
whose wife is forever lost,

by whom you used to be bossed
with anger when she was crossed.

A WEIRD SORT OF DIALOGUE, GOING WHERE?

Is life only a thing of wonder?

Sure, be my guest, start wondering about it.

For a start, what's life's definition?

A functioning organic animation.

That's too unrevealing. Is there more to it?

Probably, but my mind isn't up to it.

What's the matter, that you fall short?

Mental limitation.

Is that your fault?

Sure. It's an aspect or condition of living.

If you call it that, sure. Be my guest.

Stop being problematical.

Is that what I'm being? I wasn't aware of it.

Is this a contest between your evaluating me and my evaluating you?

Sure, you can call it that.

Are we playing?

Only verbally.

Of course. Isn't this a dialogue?

Yes. We're both full participants.

We needn't prove our credentials.

A ONE-SIDED DIALOGUE

Now I'm so more old,
I'm much less bold,
so when challenged to a fight,
I sure take flight,
like a timid bird
who responds to a shout heard
by flying away
to avoid the fray.

If you're that old, are you weak?

I've already surpassed my peak
and begun to go downhill
preparatory to death's chill.

Is that against your will?

Of course. I'd like to stay alive
in youth's condition to be able to strive,
or at least be in middle age
enough to fly beyond my cage,
and fool around with mobility
to test my remaining ability.

EXPLORING VARIOUS SUBJECTS

Death is really bad news. It creates funerals, grief, mournings, elegies, tears, burials, obituaries, and other results, leading to a negative bottom line, full of loss and regret.

You sure do give death a bad press, which it well deserves and merits, on the debit side.

Does death have a redeeming side?

It includes bad people on its elimination list.

That proves that dark clouds can grow silver outlines.

You mean "linings."

I always did bad in art, including silhouettes.

A lot of art featured illuminated outlines in putting a pretty frame over the glowing presence of theologically famous mythological creatures.

Yes, art spoke visually eloquently.

Art is to the eyes what music is to the ears.

That analogy is poetic.

Deeply emphasized outlines in art meet their equivalence in rhymes that decorate the ends of poetic lines.

How does poetry relate to art?

Through being mutually creative.

But some attempted art and poetry fail.

Their failures are counterbalanced by genius.

Can somebody be a self-proclaimed genius?

Sure, if vanity triumphs over mediocrity, and gullible people believe him or her.

I'm glad you added "or her."

Let's not make gender controversial.

You're too late. It already is.

ATTEMPTS AT DEFINING LIFE

Can you summarize or define Life, in a nutshell?

It's that without which we wouldn't be alive.

But that's an evasive definition, which precludes spilling the beans on Life's essential essence.

Life is so multivarious with its miscellany of aspects as to virtually defy definition.

To pronounce it, it's not a jawbreaker, being monosyllabic. But contained within its kernel is a certain structural magnificence.

Stop evading the issue. What's Life?

It's what Death ends.

That more defines Death than Life.

Are they enemy antagonists?

They're polar opposites. Death, being Life's loss, contains the secret of Life, within its hidden interior.

Can you break it open?

No. Life guards itself.

How? Is it some shy beast?

No. It's elusively subtle, like a product of ancient alchemy.

Stop being occultly mysterious. Are you an espionage spy with a diplomatic mission of obscurity?

No. I'm under nobody's payroll.

Then is money the answer to Life?

Only with financial due respect.

"NUTS AND BOLTS" DEFINITIONS

What's the definition of Life?

An organism's pre-death condition of biological animation.

That seems like a negative definition, when "Death" is thrown prominently into the formula.

It's a way of looking at it.

Does Death *surround* Life?

No. It only *follows* Life.

Then what came *before* Life?

Its creation.

What creation?

Like sex or some other form of reproductive propagation.

Now we're getting into mysteries.

We were there already.

How do we get out of them?

By shutting up.

Does Evolution explain the mysteries?

If so, Evolution has a large load to carry.

To Religion will it ever marry
as co-sponsors of Creation?

No. They have a mis-spent relation.

DEALING WITH A FEAR-OF-DEATH PROBLEM

I'm too afraid of death. Fearing it is my problem.

Why? Death doesn't pinch or bite you or stick a concretely sharp needle in you. The dreaded sensation of physical pain is entirely absent.

It leaves me with nothing substantially substitutional. It's a sterile empty wasteland. I'm too impatiently greedy to withstand death-fear's withholding state of barren insufficiency, a parody of minia-turism.

You'd be in your ideal element if only it were ghostly Halloween time.

But Halloween occurs only once a year. When it's over, I'd have to wait a whole year for next year's Halloween. It's too long a wait for me humanly to hold out from one Halloween to the next.

It requires iron-bound discipline that seems currently beyond you, even in your frantically accelerated death-fear emergency.

Then what cure is possible?

Resort to a stiff upper lip like a traditionally stoical Englishman.

That's impossible to fake. My acute Brooklyn accent is too pronounced.

FOR JIMMY STAGNO

Jimmy, you're dead and I'm not.
We had never known such inequality,
and it's awful.
I almost wish we could both reverse
and trade our unequal roles.
But I love myself too much
to be so self-disloyal.
You were my best pal for eighty years,
from early adolescence to my tears.
We played a lot of ball, humbly.
But you became professional.
We shared being Yankee fans,
sometimes in their glory days,
from DiMaggio to Mariano Rivera.
You had five kids, and I none.
We shared Brooklyn poverty.
In school, I was the bright one,
and for you, the right one.

So were you for me.
That's enough, Jimmy.
If we go on, I succumb to melancholy.
Without you, it's hard to be jolly,
the way we were in the old days.
So many a smile would we raise.
Thus we would share humor
in the role of double consumer.
Oh, to be a resumer
is beyond our reach.
We're separate, each from each.

EQUALITY, IN A MANNER OF SPEAKING

Are you still worried about death?

Sure. It's on the wrong side of my life.

How?

It comes *after*. Since I'm aging fast, I have little to look forward to. But if I already got death over with *before* life, then I'd feel safe and secure for the future.

Sorry. Your rearranging scheme is too unrealistic to work. It's existentially impractical, in the biological sense.

I'm a self-proclaimed idea architect.

That definition fits you. Welcome to the real world.

You mean welcome to my death?

How much time is left?

With terminal cancer and ninety years, not much.

I'm in better shape and younger, so accept my pity.

What good will it do me?

None. It was just a courtesy.

What good will your courtesy do?

It's a matter of manners.

But manners are mere ornament compared to life's basic nitty gritty.

They smooth out our fellow humanity with the pretense of equality. Now we're closer to an equal basis.

You command my greater envy.

Don't demean my competitive superiority.

LIFE IN A NUTSHELL

Life is one thing after another.

That's too simplistic a description.

Then how would *you* define life?

It's seen in retrospect. We depend on memory for a rear view of life, via recall.

Some people see life from a futuristic point of view: Being ambitious of wanting things in our future. Desiring goals.

I guess life is multi-faceted.

It has three recognized time frames: past, present, and future.

Let's congratulate each other for seeing it multi-dimensionally.

All our observations, when put together, add up to a coherent view of life in a nutshell.

Nutshells are what squirrels discard—they're refuse—mere garbage.

Stop diminishing our accomplishments. Be proud of them.

But you're "nuts" to degrade squirrels. They have amazing climbing abilities.

So what? Nature is down to earth.

What about birds?

They're too flighty.

FALLING DIALOGUE, FEATURING TWO ACROBATIC OLD MEN

Is life one thing at a time?

That description makes life seem too one-dimensional. You have to emphasize its rich complexity.

I apologize for over-simplifying life's bewilderingly miscellaneous variety.

Just even thinking about it overcomes me with confused agitation.
It gives me *ver*tigo,
so I don't know *where* to go.

Are you about to faint?

Maybe, but catch me before I hit the floor.

Thanks for your confidence in my alert ability to act quickly in an emergency to nimbly guard you against accidental fainting.

But it hasn't happened yet. Should I feint to faint?

Then I'll put on an act to catch you before you hit the floor.

If you're not on time, our double act will descend into one big flaw.

We'll end up sprawled on the ground
as an anti-climax, pound for pound.

Get up from the dusty floor
and fall for this conclusion: it's one big flaw.

I hope the audience will fall for it,
and the two of us will crawl for it.

How quaint we end up on the stage,
considering our combined age.

DEATH HAS THE LAST LAUGH.
I'M NOT SAVED BY STAYING OUT OF THE DRAFT.

Is my life wretched?
I struggle.
Is my throat hoarse?
I gargle.
Thus for each pain, I have a clue
as to what in the world to do.
Do I have remedies? A few.
My generation is dying out,
and I myself have lost the bout
to Death, having relinquished doubt.
I join in the great emptiness
that envelops my given-up soul.
There's nothing to restore me to make me whole.
Thus I'm abandoned, without a goal,
and lost in the great beyond.
Nothing remains, of which I used to be fond.

WHERE DID MY FRIENDS GO?
I'M SO OLD THAT I OUGHT TO KNOW.

My friends are lost to death,
the whole bunch out of breath
with lungs in disrepair
to remind me of despair.
Thus I'm forced to be alone.

Beyond the reach of telephone
or E-mail's useless script,
they've all without mercy slipped.
My range of popularity has dipped.
Memory lacks the vivid force
to take re-enactment's desperate course
to revive my old friends in a mass
or singularly before me to pass
skeletonically off the planet.
Such a tragedy, I didn't plan it.
A fate like this I'd never condone.
Others have it, it's not my own
groaningly to make continuous moan.
To that pass, age has seen me grown.
My longevity passed them by.
They're swept beyond into a lost sky.
I'm reluctantly forced to say goodbye
in such a muted tone
as to emphasize being alone,
barking my phlegm into a telephone
that ordinarily is silent.
The mood I'm in? It's violent.

WHEN DEATH CONTINUES TO PERSIST,
I SOMEWHAT BRAVELY STILL RESIST.
STUBBORN HABIT GIVES ME AN ASSIST.

When old age drags me down
into the precincts of Death,
I take alarm, afraid to lose
the life I felt free to choose.
All my habits expect more of the same,
though I'm too old to flirt with any dame,

for fear of bringing my masculinity to shame.
At the sight of a dame I start to drool,
and saliva falls from my dentures in a pool.
My breath is so rancid and foul,
and I lack the reputed wisdom of an owl.
Altogether, my faults pile on high,
providing evidence it's time to die.
But still I resist, stubborn and stiff.
When Death calls, I plead with him, mouthing "if."
Impatiently, Death pulls away
and makes a brutal date for another day.
Thus my life continues to resume,
although ferocious Death threatens to loom,
combing the gathering dust with a broom
and then applying a wet mop to the whole room
to cleansify the well predicted gloom.
By now, Death had gotten fed up
with all this notorious delay,
cheerfully announcing, "Let's call it a day!"
However, it turned out to be more than that,
Death rejoicing in the tit for tat.

**HAVING REACHED THE END,
I YIELD AND BEND.
MY BODY USED TO BE STRAIGHT
WHEN THINGS WERE STILL GREAT.**

I find myself about to die,
with energy not in great supply.
What I remember is in vague unrest,
and before me I'm supposed to pass what test?
My long longevity is ebbing out,
with youth so far in arrears,

that prominently to the forefront come my fears
spreading over my senior years
like a well advancing plague
whose origins remain chemically vague.
Death means only nothingness in the elastic mind,
whose free association is deaf and blind.
Thus, corrupt decay creeps up behind.
My body is falling to pieces,
and inner cohesion undergoes releases.
This is hardly an endorsement of coming death.
After vascular pains, it surrenders breath,
which used to be in the abstract
before it became my final fact.
Goodbye to the mostly unknown earth
that plays opposite role to my innocent birth.

WE'RE SUCH A GREAT PAIR, STEP ASIDE AND GIVE US AIR, OR JUST ENVY US AND STARE.

Passionately singing for us,
life breaks out in a chorus
of melodious voices
to preserve our dear choices,
begging fate or fortune
to conserve our fair portion
of life that preciously remains
with time enough to enjoy our gains
of sufficient health and money
to kiss and comfort love's dear honey,
in other words, each other,
whom too much love can't smother.
Death for yourself and her

is deep on the list of what not to prefer.
If in danger, immediately break into a stir
and work hard for security
to continually bless her and me
as far as our shining views can see
in sweet mutual arms,
resisting all possible harms.
If not, alert our alarms
to protect such double charms.
May me and my honey endure, to live
in reciprocal games of take and give.
So let's live in ideal bliss,
and add new meaning to our kiss.
If ever we get into a flare,
we'll get divorced, if we dare,
and risk the misery of despair.
If things come to such a pass,
how did we contrive to be a double ass?

ONCE YOUR FULL LIFE IS OVER, YOU'RE NOT ALLOWED A "DO-OVER."

Life is only one to a customer.
That's all I get at birth,
in the deal that keeps me down to earth.
So when I die, I can't replace me.
In no second mirror can I face me.
A second life to save me
can't be *me* again, bravely.
I look to see where I had landed,
but my ghost was seen to be abandoned,
which squeezed me dry and out of breath
for any fresh breathing after brand new Death.

So for a second time yelping,
having already had one helping,
I once again sorely reckoned
that if by nostalgia beckoned,
I'd had my turn, so couldn't get a second,
nor in a minute, and nor an hour.

DON'T WAKE MY LOVE AND ME UP AFTER WE'VE HAD A ROWDY SUP.

My lovely darling is sleeping,
so forgive me for peeping.
How well is she keeping?
In her softly steady breathing,
up and down goes her skin,
settling my image quiet within.
Let her dream modestly of me
as her soul's custodian to set us free,
as I quietly adjust my arms
not to inflict bodily harms
on her well pajama'd charms,
if I dare to slip an elbow
to poke her on some soft spot
that I often visited a lot.
But then I awake because I have to pee,
so to the bathroom I go sneakily,
interrupting this domestic scene,
slightly dozing in the obscene.
The rumpled pillows and covers
reveal us frankly to be lovers.
Insomnia can be an aphrodisiac
when two such bodies are in the sack.
We have so many dreams to unpack.

MY ODE TO MEMORY:
MY DEAR FRIEND, NOT ENEMY.
OH, I'VE FORGOTTEN SO MANY,
GRATEFUL TO REMEMBER ANY.

Memory keeps track
of what happened way back,
juggling this date with that.
We replay all those events,
but not in their proper sequence.
Some names are forgot.
But basically you get the drift.
Memory is your reminder in thrift
of what really took place
for you to confront and face,
joining your current age
with that ancient previous page,
to keep the record straight
of these reminders sadly late.
I just reach back and wait.
They drift along, at considerable weight,
but get lighter as I reach them.
Once regained, I preach them.

LIFE'S DATED VALIDITY
ADDS TO OUR TIMIDITY
BY LASTING SO LIMITEDLY.

Death is the worst thing that could ever happen to a human being.

Why?

Because it translates that former human being into a worthless non-person, who has no validity whatever.

I agree. Writers and politicians, who sought worldly fame by way of their successful accomplishments, can only realize that fame during life itself. Once dead, their fame is invalidated for themselves, because they no longer have "selves."

Life is a self? If no life, then no self?

Yes. So monuments are absurd.

Are you insulting those sculptors who used granite or marble to immortalize former objects of renown?

Yes. The sculptors are dead, in their turn.

The way you talk, the world is a huge urn
that only death will let us earn
after a uniform burn.

Your critique is so stern!

NO, IT'S TOO LATE NOW
TO REKINDLE OUR OLD VOW.

You're in my heart forever
from those good old days
on which dear emotion preyed.
Let's revive them and be jolly,
having regarded our friendship as holy.
We both remember each other wholly.
So I looked you up in praying chance
that we'd resuscitate our romance
and creakingly duplicate our dance.
Perhaps we'll revive us, perchance,
and go so far as to remarry
if we didn't already too late tarry.
How much weight do those days carry?
Maybe not enough to risk the heartbreak

if well the new effort turned out fake.
So let's leave well alone, for our mutual sake,
rather than, like photography, do another "take,"
which will only be in a quick flash
unworthy of trying another dash.
Sorry. Those days went smash
and burned themselves down to an ash.
The question I have to ask
is: how can we put on a new mask?
Impossibility mocks this task.
So let the past fade away
and put its old toys out of play
into dust-concealed storage,
despite a slight remaining adoring
I can't be heartlessly ignoring.

LET PAST LOVE ALONE
TO CHEW ON ITS STERILE BONE?
YES. A NEW LOVE I'LL HONE.

The love we used to have
stopped in its tracks,
and we can't look back.
Then why do we frequently recall it?
What disaster befell it?
More importantly, how can I quell it?
How sentimentally romantic
to make old love still tick!
No, it fell by the wayside,
and only in my heart can reside.
Yours too? Then it's not too late.
Quickly, let's scurry up another date!
Perhaps we're tampering with fate.

With what can our past equate?
Only by itself alone.
Like a dog, gnaw on this bone.
If you can't ignore it, chew some more
and risk breaking your doggish jaw.
What are we so hustling for?
To rustle up this sterile bore?
No, at one time we did adore.
That's what this pain is for.
But love is a faded old joke.
From its misery death, don't poke
to have it be awoke.
It's already been replaced,
so keep it blank, fully erased.

**YES, FOR OLD TIMES' SAKE,
THOSE OLD DAYS LET'S REMAKE,
THAT WE CLUMSILY CAME TO BREAK.**

Remembering you, dear friend,
I thought those days would never end,
how we used to roust around together
with jolly laughter and other
keen manhood emotions.
Then we foolishly drifted apart,
misplacing our friendship art.
The time appeared to be ominous
of not a word from either one
of old buddies' exchange.
Were you in fact dead,
or had I lost my head?
To investigate I was bred.
I looked you up in dread.

There you were, spankingly alive,
intensely groovy and ready to thrive!
Let's all those sacred days revive!
So on appointment, we pulled up up cheer
and brought old times closingly near,
with a meal reinforced by beer,
rejoined so shockingly close
to what we remembered the most,
though having grown so grisly
in an interim eternally busy
to temporarily strike us dizzy.
Our wives of course distracted us,
and children into the fuss.
How much time had elapsed?
We both would have collapsed.

"BETTER THEM THAN ME,"
IF DEATH UNDERGOES A SPREE

Someone else's death
doesn't hit you hard
as the one yourself will have to undergo
in its sheer fear.
How well did you know
that sculptor who had to "go"?
Very well, we were real friends.
But meeting others' ends
seems impersonal and vague,
verging on the abstract,
as under a leased contract.
I regret to see him go,
I'm saddened at his loss.
But *myself*—that's the real one

who matters to me the most.
So let's give me a preliminary toast
for having lasted a whole lifetime.
How will my mourning friends feel
once to Death I've had to kneel
and with a thud collapsed
when my tenure's lapsed?
My mortality will remind them
of their own they're yet spared.
But mainly somehow they cared
for me, whose end I've recently nightmared,
forecasting my front billing
in headlined Death's sensational killing.

THE IMPERFECT MEMORY
DAWDLES INTO INACCURACY
TO BECOME TRUTH'S ENEMY.
THUS, WHEN I EMBELLISH,
I BOAST A NEW FLOURISH.

All the things that come to be
in the realm of personal event
potentially get caught in memory's web,
but not strangle me, I hope,
in the past's overwhelming scope.
With their miscellaneous sprawl,
I can't recapture them all
in a neat and tidy pile
to carefully file
them in the brain's cabinet
broken into categories.
They recapture some of my glories
which I exaggerate into stories

to simplify the almighty past
free of amnesia's forgetful grasp.
Selectively, what happened to me
undergoes distortion and sets me fancy free.
Did that all belong to the former me?

NINETY, AND READY TO QUIT. I'LL PACK IN A BOX MY REMAINING WIT, AND PRIMARILY MY ACTIVITY IS TO SIT.

What's left of me
is ready to be free
from the shackles of "duty."
I've served my life's ambition
and run out of ammunition
to further prolong my "destiny."
The book already written,
published or not, is hard-bitten.
I drag my youth behind
with a body all used up.
Sex is in the past,
and I'll wrap it up, fast.
Goodbye, folks, thanks for the show.
I'll hang on as best I can
and eke out my diminishing "plan."
What is it, precisely?
No, I dance away nicely.

A MEMORIAL ESSAY
ON WHAT MEMORY WILL SAY.
HURRY, IT WON'T ALWAYS STAY.

Memory is like a library
of events instead of books.
There are many shelves
of all your past selves,
so you go through the aisles
racked up in neat files
to pick up past smiles
and also multiple frowns,
and humor like clowns.
They're all in your own head
to compile before you're dead.
You open up the hoard.
How can you ever be bored?
They actually happened to you,
so how could they not be true?
It's all there to refer to,
in case you want to look something up
while you pour yourself a cup
of the strong stuff or merely tea,
to fondly remember an occasion of glee.
All this will compel nostalgia
to cure you of potential neuralgia
before it even starts.
They're stacked up with various charts.
Use your brains and regain your smarts.
Include memory among private arts
to give it a special slant
to pounce upon what others can't.
What's in *your* head alone
whose duplicate can't be shown,

being privately known
in certified possession
of peculiar obsession?
You've collected, so now enjoy
what death or amnesia threaten to destroy.
Avail yourself. Don't be coy.
But some experiences you share
with others, so you all bear.

WELL, GOODBYE.
IT'S BEEN LONG DELAYED,
BUT THE GAME IS UP, IT'S BEEN PLAYED.

Your widow is filled with waving leaves
waving goodbye as you leave
your life of city dwelling.
You're over ninety, spelling
demise as your only future.
You leave the world with its culture,
all your life as a city dweller.
Now your ambition has reached the cellar.
Say goodbye to your dead friends,
all met with various ends.
You're too late for amends.
You and your wife remain.
What memories will you regain
on your way out?
Your ferocious bout
ends with a weak whimpering shout,
without even a modicum of a doubt
that three strikes fairly equal "out!"
in memorable baseball lore
that youthfully came before,

in those golden days of prime
that glorified youth in its time.
Pardon me for obsessive rhyme.

DWELLING ON YOUR LAST MINUTES
OF AN IMAGINED FINISH

Now that you're past ninety years,
you're only left with future fears
and memories sliding away
from the relevant "constant present."
Medical worries consume you
on minor comparative scale.
Remarkable longevity is no help.
Everyone's younger than you.
You bear lists of perished friends.
You now join their various ends,
featuring your own shrinking future.
What will your last thoughts be like?
Which memories might dominate
your impending inevitable self-farewell
to signal the traditional knell
and add a flair of drama?
The sentence ends with a period or coma.
You die out spewing language
to frame your bodily languish,
muttering in the dark
and relinquishing your spark.
Say only your humble goodbye
for youthful mourners to have a good cry.

ENVY DIALOGUE

(Clue: Maybe the older guy is envious of the younger guy for having longer to live?)

I heard you just turned ninety. Sorry to miss the birthday party. Are you getting worried?

Of course. That's how closer I am to death, by measurable degrees.

Being doomed is no picnic. Accept my regrets.

Not so fast. I'm still here, in reasonable health. Are you pushing me?

Sorry, that was indelicate of me.

You seemed to inflict a death wish on me.

No, maybe it's *you*, who wishes me ill. Do you have a vendetta against my being so younger than you, thus being in no immediate death danger?

Maybe I do. But you earned my self-defensiveness against being so suddenly old.

I conventionally wish you to live as long as humanly possible. *(Raises a wine glass.)* Here's to your good health, with many happy returns from your glorious ninetieth.

I suspect you of being disingenuous. You make an insincere wish.

Why do you doubt my conventional good will?

Because you're a phony, and bear malice.

What right do you have to accuse me? I only wish you well.

Your hypocrisy melts in your mouth.

Stop interfering with my digestive system.

TWO-PERSON DIALOGUE
BOUND TO PUT YOU IN A FOG.
DEATH IS SUCH A SUBJECT
THAT SOME LISTENERS WOULD OBJECT,
AND THEREFORE REFUSE TO LISTEN.
GIVE ME A TOPIC THAT WILL GLISTEN..

I'm worried that I've gotten too old, thus reducing my life expectancy.

What can you do about it?

I'm too helpless to act.

Then just accept the way the matter currently stands.

But it's an intolerable proposition.

Proposition? Who's proposing?

Death, as a matter of fact.

What's your option?

Am I free to reject Death's proposition?

Decidedly not, except guarding your health, and avoiding accidents that presume too closely to the edge of fatality.

Death is a matter of *when* and *where*.

How is a factor, too.

Now you're getting dramatic
with details so emphatic,
though the end is automatic.

Yes, the "deity" deals in details.
Show how the train de-rails,
and riders' resistance fails.
Hearing this, my complexion pales,
being exposed to such morbid tales.

Sorry we had this discussion.
My heart punctures with this obstruction
that sounds too much like horrible destruction.

**ONCE DEAD, YOUR LIFE IS UNREPEATABLE,
SINCE DEATH MADE SURE ITWOULD BE DELETABLE.
THIS TIDE OF NEGATIVITY IS UNBEATABLE.**

Life is just one for a lifetime.
Any attempt to repeat it is a crime.
"Heaven" was invented by religion,
an absurd notion shitted by a pigeon,
whose inside is so full of waste,
so deposited on benches to give our eyes foretaste.
Too bad your one lifetime can't be repeated
after its normal time on earth Death has deleted.
If there's a successful formula, it must be secreted
by some occult cult of mysticism
whose operators must perhaps face prison.
Maybe they advocate collective suicide,
which would reduce slightly humanity's tide
in this impossible world with circumference so wide
as to be augmented by paid space ride.

**DEATH CUTS OUT THE CRAP,
AND SHOVES ME OFF THE MAP.
I PRETEND IT'S ONLY A NAP,
FROM WHICH TO EASILY AWAKE
TO EAT MY BIRTHDAY CAKE.**

I'm an easy cinch
to submit to Death's pinch.
Old age has mellowed me down
to be anointed with Death's crown.
My body is so far weakened
that Death's opportunity has peakened,
and I easily fall in his lap
so that the two of us overlap,
and he shouts, "Let's cut out this crap!
If it's going to be done,
let's not be coy and pretend it's fun.
Now I'll give you a sugary pill
(making as if you're ill),
to lumpingly swallow
into your endless hollow,
knowing nothing's about to follow.
So take my lead,
and don't bother to plead.
Life was full of need,
but that's behind you,
needless to remind you!"
So I obediently absorbed this cue,
to enter the realm of no discernible view.

A RECKONING UP,
BUT CAREFULLY NOT WRECKING,
BEING OLD BUT STILL HAVING TIME LEFT,
HAVING BEEN WISELY KEPT.

My experiences straightened themselves out
into a lifetime,
and in sum that's the extent
of how my life went.
Now a reckoning has arrived
to determine if I thrived.
It's that part of my life to look back
and see if I had kept track.
How did I convert the opportunities
into acceptable continuities
that habitually repeated themselves
to wring different sounds from similar bells?
What did my life come down to
and resound itself into?
This summing up
overflows my cup.
What rearrangements will the future hold,
if I'm to make myself so bold,
and warm the future's unknown coldness?
Does it require venturesome boldness?
Now that reckoning is being kept,
what will I clean up and reject?
It all depends on how I reflect.
Thus the future is hanging
on the very wall I'm banging.

INVESTIGATING DEATH CAN BE CARRIED TOO FAR FOR THE RETURN TRIP BACK TO LIFE.

Fear of Death is a prelude to the "real thing,"
which it never actually resembles.
Nothing in life resembles Death,
which invincibly is beyond comparison.
So if you want to know what Death feels like,
the reply is that it has no feeling,
not even for itself.
So Death can only be imagined,
which has no basis of comparison.
Fear won't provide the answer.
So if you're investigating "the real thing,"
don't try it, or you'll never return
to review or perhaps edit your findings.
Curiosity killed a cat,
and it can kill you, if you go too far
in unwise investigation,
like the naturalist who visited the jungle,
but it proved to be a fatal bungle,
when a lion taught him how to tumble.
Thus the pursuit of knowledge
should self-limit to a college.
Death is in another Dimension,
which safely I ought to mention.

HOW DID LIFE TREAT YOU? VERY GLAD TO MEET YOU.

Have you played your best card
before becoming an old-age discard?
While urgent youth pressed you,

did you get good fortune's rescue,
and play out your life charmingly
to win the world disarmingly,
before your "invitation to the dance"
prove mixed results in your chance?
Now you leave life in a deep trance.
Goodbye to all your former friends,
having shared amazingly similar ends.
Thus humanity made you kin,
shuffling between loss and win.
Thus life is a mixed bag.
You may mourn, but also brag.

DEATH IS A DENIER
OF MY PETITION AS HIS DEFIER.

Life is only one to a customer.
I so valued it, I asked for a "repeat."
But Death sharply said, "No,
stick by the rules.
Don't be one of those fools
who requests a do-over.
It's not in the books
that I give concessions to crooks.
I'm Death, so I'm hard-boiled,
after all these years I've toiled.
So sorry, I deny your demand.
No one's allowed a second life
to follow precisely his first one.
I reappoint your continued doom
at my severe command,
to take effect immediately.
Then I seek new victims expediently."

Thus Death eliminated my second term,
so I remained done in.
Justice just had to win.
I was allowed no spin.
I got an official "deprive,"
permissible by point of law,
so I'm no longer alive,
as I was so beautifully before.

WHERE DOES NOSTALGIA COME FROM? FROM THE PAST, YOU DUMB BUM.

Nostalgia is our path to the past,
which otherwise doesn't last.
It operates like gasoline
which fuels the past's eternal green.
Such a green will never die,
as long as a tear creeps from the eye
to melt on my wrinkled cheek.
I renew it punctually every week.
But I cry so much, it makes me weak.
Oh, to revive the golden past
where nostalgia actually comes to life,
and time is wrenched back to its old self,
rather than shrunken photos on a creaky shelf
in an old house visited before
by my old mess of pals
of golden boys and sexy gals.
Being about to die,
amnesia blocks my wizened eye
and stifles the remarkable past
from renewing itself in one wild blast
in which all memories are cast.

Before you lose them, revoke them fast,
and treat them as souvenirs
guarded by rear guard soldiers with spears,
which children used to play with,
when each day was a renewed myth.
Now old age has shallowed me
into a past tiny and wee.
Let nostalgia reverse these odds,
and renew acquaintance with the old gods.

YOUTH AND AGE FIGHT IT OUT IN A GROSSLY UNEVEN BOUT. WHICH HAS THE MORE CLOUT?

Old age is a weak joke
that inspires condescension
and indulgent pity.
Youth is slickly witty.
The older you get,
the more life is a losing bet.
Feeling inferior to others
destroys self-confidence.
Old age closes down
like a painfully unfunny clown.
The dignity of an old man
is a myth and a sham,
and is culpably damned.
Youth is a vibrant vitality
proudly toying with energy
that's self-renewable
and easily chewable.
Old age huffs and puffs
with ever diminishing stuffs

that crumble into trash,
or embers composed of fire's ash.
Let's give pity to old age,
and shuffle him soon off the stage
before too much compassion is required,
as to make youth neurotically wired.

DOES TIME COUNT? AND HOW!
BUT WHAT IF IT GIVES OUT?
WELL, THAT'S WHAT IT'S ALL ABOUT.

Obsessed with death due to my old age,
and weakened by bodily accumulation
of disease and infirmity,
I allow myself (as if I had a choice)
to be dragged deathwise,
to face the approaching non-surprise,
in helpless obedience
to labor-saving expedience.
I'm doomed. No nonsense about it.
I have an indefinite date with Death,
despite doctors whom we depend on.
They do their jobs and get their salary,
while I'm driven to Death Alley
in a car rescued from the junk.
This is a theory which I can't debunk,
so close to reality's existence
that my unknown date doesn't require persistence.
Death will be as natural as Nature,
along with its unfancy nomenclature.
I'll be featured as its object,
in no condition to object.
I'll be featured as its subject,

an obligation to which I'm subject.
So Death and I will be a team.
Cancellation is only a dream
that precedes the actual event,
whose occurrence will meet complete extent.

DEATH COULD HAVE BEEN WORSE, BUT MERCY REDUCES ITS CURSE.

To lose life is to lose everything,
but otherwise things are fine.
Too bad you can't dine,
and drink a little wine,
but at least you're not suffering.
So death could have been worse,
but mercy makes it quite neutral,
even though nothing looks beautiful.
Death could have been much worse,
but it's spared you from the hurts.
Ideally, you would have liked flirts
in whom to be immersed,
and break through with an erotic burst.
So at least you're not in torment
at this particular moment,
so no harm is soon meant
bearing malicious intent.
Death appears like a harmless, timid gent.
So let's return to neutral,
where nothing is beautiful.

LIVING LIFE STRAIGHT

How do you explain life?

I'm not an expert analyzer. As far as life is concerned, all I do is live it. I'm too intuitive to follow a blueprint. Life is what I do.

Yes, but you have an intellect.

That's on the side.

But isn't intellect on the forefront of living, not just a sideline?

I'm a man of action.

Does that include being an anti-intellectual?

Not at all. You'd be surprised at how interesting some of my thoughts are.

Is it like being a walking movie?

Yes, but sometimes I sit down, just like in a regular movie.

Do you eat popcorn?

Doing things simultaneously comes easy. It's a money saver.

You're observing economy?

No, I'm practicing it.

You sure got life figured out.

I let *it* do the work. It figures *me* out.

I hope it's not deluded.

No. I'm honest.

How do you know?

I'm trustworthy.

FRED AND ME

Poor Fred.
He's dead.
But not me.
I'm free
to still be.
So I'm the lucky one,
but not for long.
To me I'll be addressed
by mourners, "So long,"
accompanied by no song.
I won't be there to reply,
already occupied by being dead,
just like my old friend, Fred.
I'm not dead *instead*,
but we're in the same boat,
which thus refuses to float.

[*Note: the artist Fred Gutzeit (1940–2022) was a good friend, whose studio Marvin visited in 2012 as part of a series of Vimeo interviews (a transcript appears in* Life's Tumultuous Party) *and for whose exhibition "SigNATURE" Marvin wrote an introduction.*]

DOGGED ENOUGH TO KEEP YOUR DOG FROM BOLTING AND BARKING UP THE WRONG TREE, WHICH IS JOLTING

I love life, but I get too old to keep it, because death loves to feast on the aged.

Then you're in a fix. Why don't you concentrate on how bad life sometimes makes you feel, so you'll be able to tolerate death by comparison?

Emphasize the negative? No thanks! I won't sabotage my valuable love of life. I'm loyal to it.

Then be resigned to have to lose what you so dearly love.

But that's unacceptably tragic. Life is my sweet dear pet.

Well, keep it on a leash, so it won't run away.

I'm so old that I'm too weak to hold my pet Life on a tight enough leash to stop him from breaking away forever.

Then hug your dog to death.

No, I hug him *from* death.

Make up your mind. Death is in only one direction.

Yes, it's a *dog*matic cur.

COMPARING FEAR WITH THE REAL THING

My fear of dying has reached a pathetic extent.

Fear?! Wait till you're forced to face the real thing!

You mean death itself? That's too morbid. It's intolerable.

Well, then, accept fearing, which is small-fry and puny compared to the real thing.

They both stink.

But fearing is relatively harmless. It's preferable. You're still alive, at least.

I fear you're right.

CHARACTERS: TWO OLD MEN

How I love life! How I dread losing it!

Those two go together. The older you get, the more in love with life, the more your danger of losing it alarmingly increases.

It's a vicious cycle. What can I do to slow it up?

You're helpless. You're doomed.

I have a solution.

Desperately tell me. I'm in the same plight or fix as you, being just as old.

Get fed up with life. Get disappointed in it, so that you'll welcome its escape.

No. That's betraying what I love. It's too self-defeating.

In that case, resign yourself and give up. You're in a tragic fix. It's not comic material.

Absolutely not. I won't include it in my nightclub act, as a stand-up comedian.

You'll be boo'ed off the stage.

Well, comedy is the other side of tragedy.

Like two sides of a coin? Here's a coin. I'll flip it to see which side turns up.

Don't be flippant.

THE DIFFERENCE BETWEEN THEN AND NOW
MAKES US BREATHLESSLY INQUIRE, "HOW?"
BUT ONLY IN RETROSPECT,
WHICH ONCE WAS BRILLIANT IN PROSPECT.

When I remember my romantic episodes,
I ask, "Where did those women go?
How did they abandon my arms
and escape with all those charms
that were so captivating
as to request their reactivating?"
But ideal moments are not forever.
Who knew that we were going to sever?
Not us, in our inspired permanence
that aspired to fixed eminence
as Mister and Missus Married Couple
whose domesticity would be so double
as to avoid any later trouble.
Such ideals are not so subtle.
Now we forget each other's names
without even feeling romantic shames.

DIALOGUE OF HOW TO EXTRACT MONEY FROM
DEAD PARENTS

Legally speaking, can I sue my parents for giving birth to me when
they were virtually teenagers?

Why?

Because if they had waited longer till they were more mature, then
I'd today be much younger, and therefore would have a longer time
to still live.

I understand your reasoning. Life has a lot to do with time.

I ask you this because you've had law training.

The answer is "no," because they're now both legally dead. Therefore they're not responsible for "jumping the gun" in getting you right after legally married at too young an age to prevent you from being so old today.

But didn't they leave an estate before dying?

No. Being both dead makes them equally both irresponsible. So legally you have to remain just as poor as before.

I got a raw deal.

Well, if you need more money, get it by other means.

That reduces me to being a crook.

Well, my advice is to be silent.

What good would that be?

Then you wouldn't put your foot in your mouth.

Who would know the difference?

**IT'S ALL OVER
FOR THE FORMER ROVER.
THE ONCE LOVER
SWEPT ABOVE HER.**

Life has had its turn.
Now it's death's day
to post-complete
what life left.
The dead are always bereft
of what they used to be.
Their identities are fled
into unrecovery.
It's as if they'd never been,

buried in the garbage bin.
Thus it's: "Goodbye Life, nice to know ya.
We merit you and bestow ya
with a medal for what you've been,
buried in the garbage bin."

WHERE THINGS ARE

Where can I locate my memories?

In the past. You just have to hark back.

But I thought they were in my brain.

There too.

I'm getting geographically confused. Then where's my body?

Just below, if not a part of, your brain.

I always knew that my body was more earth-bound than my brain.

Your brain is in your head, which is in the clouds.

That's better. The sky's the limit.

That sounds top-heavy.

Don't worry. Gravity will bring it down.

To earth-level?

To the grave.

That far down?

It bottoms out.

At ass-level?

You're hitting below the belt.

You've got to know your place.

How high can I get from alcohol?

It depends on how much you pack in.

NEGATIVE LOCATION

Is Life the best blessing we can have?

Yes.

Where does that put Death?

In Nowheresville.

Sounds like a small town or even village, nominally referred to ironically. Where is it located?

Like its name implies, nowhere.

That sounds like it's empty of substance.

You're substantially right.

Does it bear any remnant of its former resident?

Not a hint. He was struck off the map.

Was there even a map?

No, it was too irrelevant. Why take up usable space?

But Nature abhors a vacuum.

Death is only on Nature's downside.

RENEWING PAST PLEASURES BY MEMORY ALONE

I'm racing against death to hurry up and remember my fondest nostalgic memories before death blots them away forever.

Oh, you want to review them again before it's too late. But is that the best way to spend your pre-death time?

Yes, they were my chosen top events. I'll enjoy them all over again, even with a tinge of sadness that they're merely recollections.

Then I accuse you of living in the past.

What's wrong with that? It's my pleasure.

But not a *living* pleasure. In food's terms, it's like reheating remnants of a previous meal.

They could still be delicious. Reheated food at least is real in the mouth. But relived memories are too remote.

Oh, stop being fastidious. Get your renewed pleasure whenever and however. If you can still drag second-hand pleasure out of the however distant past, do so, despite that accompanying tinge of lingering sadness.

You always were a hedonist.

REVIEWING THE RESULTS

In life, have your pleasures outnumbered your pains?

I haven't kept strict personal archives, and my mathematical resources fall short of my precise recollections.

So much of life remains tinged in mysterious vague darkness?

Yes. Much of the past slips away.

Easy come, easy go?

That's a huge amount of material I've put away.

Let it go. Life is just a song.

I'm surprised you put it in vocal terms of musicality.

What were you assuming?

That you declare life as just a dream.

I did enough sleeping to call it a dream.

But most of sleeping was dream-uncollectable.

We're not accountants. Just let it go.

Just like that?

We're not hoarders. Easy come, easy go.

What about difficulties?

They did stand in my way, like so many difficulties do.

Then be accountable.

Don't load me with work. I did enough. I'm through, I'm exhausted.

Then you're complaining?

Not really. I'm just tired.

If you're not dead yet, just be glad for the extra energy.

How will I use it?

With and by whatever means.

That sounds like I'm a utility vehicle.

A biological mechanism?

The humanity version.

WITH NO TRACE OF STUPIDITY

If you're suffering from fear of death,
that's a realistic attitude,
for which you have every justification.
Time will bear you out,
and prove you stood on solid ground
to thus predict so soundly.
The evidence is all on your side
that fear will be replaced by its fulfillment,
and it's not merely a crazy belief
based on paranoid insanity.
So if you're mocked as a coward,
the mockers are harsh and cruel.

You're well within your rights
to mourn the evidence of your frights
before they ever actualize.
Life is only a temporary prize
reduced to proportion's precarious size.
Time makes the bargain slight,
gradually increasing the killer's might.
So give death enough credit
to be highly efficient of its method,
and with seemingly only slight effort,
like an apple falling from a tree
in the process of magnetic gravity.

DEATH? ALWAYS BE SUSPICIOUS THAT AT HIS HEART HE'S MALICIOUS.

You can't get out of life alive,
so you might as well not even try.
Let's investigate death with an advanced spy,
and get him to tell you the results.
We can take it, because we're all adults.
Death deprives us of what we call joy.
Its single-hearted desire is to destroy,
while sparing you if you're a young girl or boy.
Thus death is really an old softy,
and most sentimental at heart.
He's somewhat on the melodramatic side,
and is always ready to invite you for a ride.
But feel free to refuse.
If you trust him, you're bound to lose.
Pretend that you're free and easy and loose.
Act cool and nonchalant
as a defensive maneuver to charm.
Militate for a mutual truce to disarm.

IS THIS IT?
I'M SURE NOT FIT.
DO I HOLD OUT WITH WIT?

Too many repetitively scheduled definite birthdays
stack up against my one indefinite deathday.
I hold out with precarious worry
and hope the end won't hurry.
The calendar moves in a flurry.
My body weakens minute by minute.
The death panic is here, and I'm too much in it.
When will worry turn into the real thing,
as I hover near the border line
and draw the transition too fine?
At stake is the whole world that's still barely mine.
It flutters uneasily in my reached-out hand
of wrinkled tremble, sturdy and bland,
waiting for something unwillingly grand
to be put geographically off the map
to take my last untrivial nap.
I rise grandly, not like a weak sap?
No, I succumb meekly
and the calendar jolts closed
in the tremendously least and most.
Who's my ungenial host?
I reach out and become empty-handed.
Just where have I abruptly landed?
Thus I'm rhyming to the end.
Do my lines scan and blend?
If they're faulty, what can mend?
Or is everything too late
and has fallen off the slate?
Death is well nigh here,
obliterating anything formerly dear.

HERE'S HOW DEATH MOCKS.
IT TURNED OFF ALL THE CLOCKS.
THAT'S THE LEAST OF ITS HARD KNOCKS.

Avoiding death is practically a duty.
The world it gives you is shorn of beauty.
A man can't flirt with his cutie,
nor can a dame seduce a man.
Death closes up all hatches
from which the scribe can send dispatches.
Death is like a disease
whose consequences hardly please.
Nervous? You won't be put at your ease
by death's unruly ministrations.
So avoid victimization
by death's administration.
It's a fascist autocracy
that spurns your democracy.
You wish to be at liberty
with a banner under freedom?
No. Death is a slave owner,
and your captivity is a bonus.
Heaven doesn't exist,
no matter how you persist,
raising your skeletonic fist.
You tried so hard, yet you missed.
Tears will pour from your eyes,
yet heaven's failure is no surprise.
Even appealing to Jesus
resulted in a pagan leastest,
having rejected his thesis
on which the clergy feastests.
So accept death as your doom,
since heaven's landlord has no more room.

There's nowhere else to dwell,
but at least you're not going to hell.
Doesn't that ring a redeeming bell?

WHAT ABOMINATIONS DO WE DO
TO OUR OWN PASTS!
YES, BUT DON'T WORRY—
THE DAMAGE NEVER LASTS.

We dip into the past
to make what's remembered so vast
as to exalt and romanticize it.
The past thus being tampered
and indulgently pampered,
does memory make it weirder?
Yes, to the point of being theater,
and you yourself are in the audience
of your past's self-performance as fraudulence.
Then can we believe memory?
Yes, it's a friendly enemy
with what it tenders me.
It's not an exact replica,
and makes the horizontal perpendicular,
not being so particular.

HISTORY OF AN OLD MAN'S AMOROUS PAST

We mess around with our past
by applying false memory
to what actually happened or occurred.
Thus the "back-then" got blurred.
If memory were a pair of glasses,

it would disfigure the wrong loves with the right lasses,
to whom erroneously I made blundering passes.
Ultimately, did I mismarry the wrong one?
Funny how mathematically I mismanaged the whole sum.
It doesn't mean women are all alike.
Differentiate the ones you love from those you like,
who only advised you to "take a hike"
if you had tumbled off your haphazard bike.
When you recovered and came to your senses,
you fathered sons and daughters to swell up the census
through the retrospective lens
of somehow mistangled "now"s and "then"s
in the long-lost scheme of things
backwards to which memory awkwardly brings,
but then mistakenly includes some "flings"
mis-resembling the ones to whom the heart clings,
when all those women are sorted out
in priority of whom I dreamed the most about
with an involuntary passionate shout.
Thus remembering past loves,
I separate dear embraces from hasty shoves.

LIFE TRANSCENDED BY DEATH
AT THE MEDICAL CLOSE OF BREATH

When death becomes a real event
and not a terrified fear,
you've experienced your final year
in drugged-up incomprehension
that eases off the old tension
fraught with apprehension.
So now you've gone steadily
into your mourners' minds readily.

They'll escort you to the grave,
a done deed, so no need to be brave.
The wake will be a rowdy rave
in your honor. Too bad you're absent
due to your lapse of sense,
with your skull so bony dense.
You leave no spiritual soul,
with nothing tangible to console
by taking on a pseudo role.

IS TIME SO FICKLE
AS TO GET ITSELF IN A PICKLE?
SCRATCH YOURSELF TO RELIEVE YOUR TICKLE.

The past went away,
and the present has arrived.
How has this been contrived?
Mourn the vanished past
and let the present newly last
for a little while, till it's also past.
Time is always going one way.
Its victims flop behind and stray
to become so obsolete
that their life spans are complete,
which we may now delete,
due to the past being dead
as only a figment in our head.
Get your head rearranged
to accommodate what all has changed.
Don't blame time. It's not deranged.
Time dictates to the history books
to protect our reputation. We're not crooks.
But the past makes a weird comeback

as spooks who have lost track.
Time's now compelled to take a new tack.
Between the past and the now
is enough discord to confuse a highbrow.
Let's reconcile all the tenses
to comply with the general consensus.
Yet all goes on, relentless.

TO MY PAL FOREVER

Finally the goodbyes are over,
and you say goodbye for the last time,
shaking the hand of your dear old friend,
grabbing his elbow and making it bend.
Is this it? Then farewell.
It's been good to know you
through year in, year out.
Now we must say goodbye.
Pardon me if I cry.
Is this the last time?
We've been friends forever,
and wish each other well at the end.
Only in fantasy can those days return.
I sob. We'll meet in the lost land,
and then again I'll grip your hand.

INVADING DEATH'S PRECINCTS
TO RENEW OLD FRIENDS' LINKS
BY IMAGINATION'S RULE,
TO OVERCOME PROLONGED ABSENCE,
LIKE A REPEATED ABSCESS,
BECOMING INTOLERABLY CRUEL

Virtually all my old pals are dead.
Where does that leave me?
Basking in wasteful longevity,
beyond recognition by my former crowd,
even if they heard me speaking aloud
with such echoes as to bruise their ears
and release all their stored-up tears
from our being kept ruthlessly apart
after gregarious communicative art.
We all fell on each others' arms,
careful not to administer any harms
after so endlessly long apart,
so we reviewed withheld charms.
Seeing us all was a feast
on which everyone gorged, to say the least.
Thus with old friendships renewed
like one combined organic beast,
we overheard our own selves speak,
dizzy to re-climb former social peaks,
for which the restrained past nostalgically speaks.
Such remembrance we endured,
to regain lost relinquished years, secured
after painstakingly tempted and lured.

GETTING NOT LISTENED TO,
SHOULD I CONFINE MY SPEECHES TO A ZOO,
AND WONDER WHOM IS SPEAKING TO WHO?
I'M LOOKING FOR AN AUDIENCE TO WOO.

As old age arrives, I'm getting crazy,
due to mental discipline bogged down lazy.
I better soon rectify the problem,
or else slip further into the doldrum
and proceed sucking on my thumb
to signify how I've become dumb.
Let the momentary aberration recede,
so once again I'll do the right deed,
so that attention on me will feed,
and I'm socially acceptable once more,
so when I speak, I won't automatically bore,
compelling my "listeners" to fall asleep,
where in concert they proceed to snore,
as if to ask, "What is he speaking for,
other than to provoke us to have to ignore?"
Thus attention isn't granted to what I say,
so while I have the floor, listeners have drifted away.
Speaking then to an unheeding audience,
I'm granted no one to laud my grain of sense,
since I don't hold my listeners in suspense.
Is it I or they who are so accusably dense?
Am I perhaps insignificant?
Thus maybe I haven't made a dent,
despite my strenuous efforts spent?
I've always tried to be a polite gent.
Where was their attention, so bound to be lent?
I'm still waiting for them to heed,
and find their eyes wake up as I proceed.

LIFE'S ABREVIATED DESCRIPTION, AT LEAST PUTTING IT ON THE MAP, SO NOW YOU CAN TAKE A NAP.

Life is a small organically mobile island
between vast times of pre-birth
on the round face of the earth,
and vast times of post-death.
It was your own affair,
given your name and identity,
but related to relatives
along your way,
plus non-relatives though involved,
at various times.
This definition is a cold-fish attitude
without emotional input.
You were lucky to have life,
and alternately at times unlucky,
depending on how it affected you.
Well, you had your chance,
but used up all of youth allotted.
Now your old age is more than half-way plotted.
Death is your next and final stage,
due to excessive old age,
or disease or accident before.
Such was your life, to the core.
I won't describe it further
so as not to be a micro-spoken bore
with details quite safe to ignore.
This was a mini-description
categorized as non-fiction.
If I left out the details,
you don't have to go off the rails
by resorting to any number of life's available ails.

Any questions? Utilize emails,
in case my previous definition fails
to satisfy your incessant appetite
for a definition that's vividly tight
and makes you see the infinite light.

SOMETHING INDEFINABLE.
IS IT EVEN FINDABLE?

"Half in love with easeful Death,"
do I expend my last ounce of breath?
Somehow Death is a great big tease
to put me at a peculiar ease,
almost perverted somehow.
Death and I are on sexual terms,
to fool around with near poison
to drag out a hidden thrill –
from the secret recess of a pill?
(But I don't take any pill.)
Something mysterious is going on,
or is it perhaps some criminal "con"?
All this is far-fetchedly beyond me,
yet close at hand that I can't deduct,
nor with timidity detect.
Certain thoughts are not fully explained,
yet in the barrier between "obscure" and "plain."
My logical mind isn't always there.
It just goes out for a gulp of air.
Then it comes back to the familiar,
but what in the world is *that*?
Don't leave me on the verge of "abstract."
Let's formulate some convivial pact,
and somehow reverse track.

What do I somehow detect?
Is it something in the form of a defect?
What in the world am I getting at?
This is difficult to break down.
Am I a clown? Or just wanting renown?
This is a mysterious case.
How does it start at the base?

THE DEATH KISS

(1)

The death kiss,
performing the ultimate drama
with me in frail departure,
having run out of stamina,
while she retains her full glamour
in my last blind glimpse of her,
brightly resolved in a blur
of overspilling tears
to commemorate the old years.

(2)

In the last throes of being alive,
my love for my lady will survive.
I offer her a farewell goodbye
while she holds my frail hands,
and her kiss on my lips lands.
So in partnership we part,
she to the still-living side,
while I to death will abide.
Our final contact will unite
my slipping deathwise
with her remaining lifewise.

Thus me and my loving wife
from opposite ends represent death and life,
while love is the factor in between,
to be the active actor as the slate is wiped clean.
Our tears have carried over:
the doomed dead one and the lover.
We nestled briefly under that final cover.

THE BODY'S BULLYING OF THE MIND, DECIDING WHEN TO DIE

Since I get older every day, is there a cut-off point where I couldn't get any older without dying?

Yes, there's a law whereby you pay the supreme penalty for sticking around too long.

Who decides that?

Your body.

I thought I decided.

No. Your body is in charge.

But what if he's the tyrannical type, like an autocratic dictator?

Then you're under his thumb and have to obey. He'll decide when your aging has gone on too far, and when it's time for your dying to take place.

I believe in democracy.

That's just an excuse to stay alive despite a decrepitly old body.

Do I have to play by the rules?

Yes. The body rules.

That's not fair. I'm the manager.

You mean you're the brains?

Right. Aren't my brains the controller?

No. The body is the boss.

Then why did I go to school and get educated?

That was just to entertain your mind while the body was wearing itself out.

I defy the body to have bullied my mind.

Life is a game. Play by its rules.

But it's not fair.

You're prejudiced by being a brainiac.

Brainiac? Is that a creature from Mars?

LIFE CYCLE AND ITS AFTERMATH

What's life?

I don't know. But it's great living it.

Sometimes it's a lousy deal.

Well, getting born was a good risky bargain.

It sure paid off, but sometimes let me down.

Your parents were strangers to you, but had fun begetting you.

Then they owned me, and became familiar bosses of my early baby life and later.

Well, they're both dead now, and you became old.

I overdid becoming old, so the penalty is: soon I won't "be."

Not "being" defeats life's whole purpose.

That's the way it goes. Like it or lump it.

Well, wish me luck.

Sorry. Luck stops with death.

So death goes on, as if nothing happened.

Death is oblivious to your non-being, which it not only started, but perpetuated. It's pretense as if nothing happened.

What a careless interferer, not to mention disrupter!

Did you get any kid of your own?

Yeah, but where is she now?

A POEM AGAINST DEATH, TO SAVE THE READER'S VALUABLE BREATH

Life is such a wonderful asset,
that why must Death be a killjoy,
whose lone object is to destroy?
Can you imagine such complete opposites?
On one side, Life sits;
and on the other, Death lurks.
So differentiate, you jerks!
Anyone who prefers Death
has lost his brains, not only his breath.
Thus I deem that Life's a tragedy.
But I dream that Death won't be ratified
unless common decency will be applied,
and dastardly Death will be defied,
instead of perversely deified
Give Death a permanent vacation
to try a more peaceful vocation.
Where? I don't know yet the location.
But certainly not in the world's hell
that Death abets by ringing everyone's bell.
Philanthropy will eventually quell
Death's murderous greed and send him to hell.

I'd love to see Death begging for mercy
before all the judges of New Jersey.

DEATH

The longer you have to wait,
the older you get.
Hold out and escape it?
Impossible to be self-mourning:
"No bacon and eggs this morning."
Diet thins you. It's like a diet.
When death comes, you can't defy it.
Its actuality is palpable,
like Cezanne's unpolished apple
that sits roundly on the table.
Contemplate it, if you're able.
Soon your mind moves away.
That apple just won't stay.

WHAT'S ITS EFFECT ON YOU?
THE ANSWER IS: "WHO WAS IT?"

Death is the big disappearance act.
It turns into a horrible fact.
Whoever it happens to
has a different effect on you.
Most deaths you're indifferent to.
Those people didn't matter much to you.
You may have slightly regretted.
But what the hell—you let it.
Others caused you grief.
Others—to hell with them—it's a relief.

But some—you mourn dreadfully.
The vanished ones went away dead-fully.
They became another statistic.
Admit it—you were slightly sadistic.
They're no longer a nuisance.
Actually, they were a pain in the neck.
"Good riddance" is your attitude.
"Better him than me" is another.
Yourself is the one who really counts.
Accordingly, the fear of death mounts.

DIALOGUE FOR TWO OLD MEN

The older you get, the closer you are to death.

How did you figure that out? Are you a brilliant mathematician?

It's just common sense. Aging goes in contrary directions from vitality.

That statement ought to be put in a health magazine that even doctors prescribe to.

I found that out by personal experience.

What a revelation! Describe your findings.

As the years were piling up, I found myself getting so weaker that I even invested in a cane.

You cheapskate! It was about time. I hope you use it up and get your money's worth from this cane.

In my will, I left it to my son.

How far away is he from that inheritance?

From my death. To the point where he can profit from his *legacy*.

I'm glad you gave him a *leg*-up. Did he inherit the horse too?

No. The only hoarse I have is with a sore throat.

Well, our dialogue sure limped along.

Talking is a great method of conversation.

TWO LOYAL DEATHS

Death's resounding victory over Life
was the unsurprising outcome of their strife.
Life had become already much too old
to challenge Death, who was ruthlessly bold.
Being old, Life was accordingly feeble,
and succumbed, just like billions of other people.
The referee concluded that it was "no contest,"
given such a one-sided conquest,
and lifted Death's decisive hand
to end the battle that had become too bland,
due to Death's obviously having the upper hand.
Life was buried in miserable shame,
having submitted to Death's far superior game.
Death had so pulverized Life
that it led to the grief Death of Life's weeping wife.
Thus, being miserably divided,
that pathetic couple's twin Deaths almost coincided.

I CAME FULLY AROUND
THE BIRTH CYCLE AND LANDED ON THE GROUND.

Life is the sweetest gift you've ever received.
It's so magnificent, you won't believe.
You owe it to two people having sex.
They're utter strangers to you, right away.
But later they'll proudly teach you the time of day.

In adolescence you may resent them,
with youthful rebellion.
But they retaliate and keep you in order.
They won't let you slip over the border.
They paid the rent and fed you, so you owe them,
and mainly they got you an education
through the school system.
It behooved you to listen,
so later your life will glisten.
Thank you for having sex, parents.
Getting me was great. That's apparent.
Now you two are among the dead.
How lucky for me, the day you wed
so innocently for me on your virgin bed.
The life it gave me served me in good stead.
Now I've become big and famous.
I myself am venerable and old.
Soon I'll join you in the ancient fold.
I'll take the liberty, if I so make bold.
But you two got me, good as gold.

GETTING ANOTHER LIFETIME?
IS THAT A SUPERNATURAL CRIME?

Slow up the progress of your aging
till it approximates longevity's staging
of your one-man lifetime show,
that stalls to the point of being slow.
Make Death give up waiting
by falling asleep instead
of hastening your being dead.
So perhaps if Death should neglect you,
he'll never arrive when his appointment is due.

That will result in a second lifetime for you,
with extensions up to eternity.
But much of your time will be in the infirmary,
where you gasp for breath with the nurse's aid,
due to actual Death's interrupted raid.
All this is mightily extensive,
but it's bound to be otherworldly expensive.
Is there a currency exchange rate
to pay up for Death's missed date?
This sounds so very supernatural
that it's too absent-minded to be factual.
Death's delay is worth a wait
if it prolongs my out-of-this-world fate.
Anyway, I'll enjoy going in orbit.
I visit the supernatural,
while Death stays behind with a forfeit.
But doesn't it sound a wee bit morbid?
Eventually, I might get bored with it.

BORN, AND ON MY WAY
TO TAKE LIFE DAY BY DAY

Getting born as a little baby
wasn't too enlightening.
In fact, it was frightening.
I'm not entitled to that memory,
but the world appeared to be an enemy.
My first contact was my mother,
fresh from sex with my father.
My mother was the instigator
as the instant baby baiter.
(That's me whom she guided.)
Instantly, I abided.

So we two got along fine,
since she was obviously mine.
I sucked her breast for milk
as primary nourishment
and thirsty refreshment.
I got off to a good start,
and had natural ability to be smart.
Now I'm a very old man,
having negotiated all that span
in the world of adults,
having gotten good results.
However, I'm doomed by very Death
to lose all, starting with breath.
My attitude is fear
to have it so near.
My dear wife will mourn me,
and various friends.
My casual knowers may attend,
plus son and daughter.
I await my slaughter.

**YOU'RE NO LONGER "WITH IT,"
WITH ANY INKLING OF CONTEMPORARY WIT.
PERHAPS YOU'VE SWALLOWED THE WRONG BIT.**

The older you get, the more you're out of tune
with this generation's fashionable balloon.
The songs are different, and also costumes,
from what you remember in old customs.
Perhaps the world has passed you by,
since your sympathy with it is in short supply,
and young people look at you askance,
since your rhythms don't approximate the latest dance.

Where the hell do you think you are? In France?
So give up being in tune with the world,
although it's about time you gave it a whirl,
and know what to say when flirting with a girl.
You're regarded as an old-fashioned type
that's not up to date with the latest hype.
You don't hear the juicy jive that comes down the pipe.
Maybe you've had it, getting so old
that it's too late to try to seem bold.
The youth laugh at you as you pass by
in clothes of long ago.
The new modern world is your apparent foe.
They recite new poets, not Edgar Allen Poe.

FOOLISHLY WANTING A REPEAT, ONCE LIFE WAS ALREADY COMPLETE

When I died, with what was I left
in sad view of retrospect?
I reviewed my whole life's career
from the backward mirror in the rear,
from birth to infancy to youth,
to deep maturity and final truth.
What had I concluded about my life?
It went from adolescent bewilderment
to the rectitude of old age,
leading, alas, to the final stage.
That's where I gave up the ghost
and began to miss life the most.
Could I regain it with a claim
that I deserved a repeat under my former name?
No, my lifetime was only once.
To expect a return was the whim of a dunce.

**FUSS MADE AFTER MY DEATH,
SEEING MY MOURNERS RUN OUT OF BREATH.
THEY WERE EACH A DRUNKEN ROWDY
WHO RUSHED INTO MY FUNERAL TO SAY "HOWDY."**

Poor me. If Death grabs me and won't let go,
I've now become an object of woe
for a whole army of mourners
who rush to my corpse from all corners,
to congregate in despair
that my broken body is beyond repair.
They sing for me a goodbye carol,
and dump my remains in an open barrel
from which my untidy bones stick out.
The occasion deteriorates into an unruly rout,
which signifies their instigation of a wake
from which I, the celebrant, am unlikely to wake.
Thus passed the occasion improvised for my sake.
Each mourner plucks a bone
as a souvenir from the barrel to bring home,
where all the while my ghost continues to roam,
letting out an occasional scream
as residue from a nightmare dream
participated in by my mourners
who'd arrived from diverse odd corners.

**AGAINST DEATH, IN FAVOR OF LIFE.
THAT'S THE PLATFORM FOR VOTING,
WITH ALL YOUR POLITICS PROMOTING.**

Death is so terrible that everyone should avoid it.
Someone should already have destroyed it.
On the contrary, Life is so preferable

that its influence exceeds the ineffable.
So therefore your choice is obvious.
Life receives the popular vote.
To its cause, everyone should devote.
If anyone is dead, he should promote
his defunct corpse to Life again
for renewed substance. Being dead is unsubstantial,
since all it could do is really stand still,
as if the corpse were already terribly ill.
So our motto should be "Revive:"—
a key essential to the paradise of "Survive."
"Survival" becomes a dynamic word,
rendering all other vocabulary absurd.
So concentrate on coming back to Life,
with the auxiliary clause of avoiding strife.
Make renewed Life as easy as possible,
to contradict doubters who claim it impossible.

THE SPEECH DIALOGUE, BY TWO OLD MEN

Is life worth holding on to, even though it's the mere dregs of our former selves?

Yes, as long as you haven't reached the "it's too much pain" level.

Remaining within the precincts of your "comfort zone" is a necessary factor to keep up life's indomitable will.

You sure did say a mouthful.

I've kept up my "gift for the gab."

It keeps up the gates of conversation from going the way of all flesh.

You're wrong in your metaphor, due to gates being made of metal or wood or stone, *not* of flesh.

Thanks for correcting the material in my metaphor.

Flesh is for *going through* the gates.

I always wondered what it was for.

Speech is such a valuable aspect, we'd have to support its well-being.

Without speech, where would communication be?

Out the back door.

NOTHING MORE REAL OR TRUE
APPLIES DESCRIPTIVELY TO THE FORMER YOU.
YOU'RE BEING COMPLETELY IGNORED
BY THE NEW GENERATION (SO BORED!)

Heaven simply doesn't exist,
so you might as well not persist.
Give up its futile search,
and also your place on earth,
which used to be guaranteed.
But you can't go on. The farmer pulled up your weed.
Thus the former you
is no longer real or true.
You're only a bunch of bones
into which you lived like little homes,
allowing your mentality to occasionally roam,
when on your brow you had a thinking dome.
Now death has plowed you under,
so there's nothing more to wonder.
Let the infernal rains thunder.

THE BLESSED EVENT

When life is issued into being by fertile parental sex, it seems to come with a proviso that death must come at the end of the trail or trial. The born baby, of course, has no inkling of this proviso, which would be a killjoy or comfort-spoiler if notably noted. The proviso is an "elephant in the room," which is ignored, so as not to spoil the celebrated birth event in the "feel good" atmosphere of birth-sanctifying.

Much later, after a full lifetime, the proviso comes to root. The"promise" is fulfilled.

Meanwhile, a new generation has settled in. "Time flies" is everyone's accepted conclusion, since cliches are hard to change.

"Welcome to the world, little one." Meanwhile, the parents are beaming through exhaustions of exhileration, congratulated by assembled onlookers.

HERE'S MY REMAINING FATE.
IT'S NOT QUITE FIRST-RATE.

What's next on my agenda,
having to be life's spender,
with no more prospect of splendor
except the option to surrender?
I've squandered my entire youth,
leaving old age to be my final truth.
Can I protest? No, I'm mute.
After all this, then what's left?
The dubious privilege of being bereft.
Wonderful times happened to me.
But now my rusty ghost yearns to be free.
Medically I've so deteriorated
that my chances of survival are nil-rated.

To doom and Death I'm fated.
Will future hope make me elated?
No. Things are even worse than stated.
If I'm still pleading for the element of hope,
I should give up, unless I'm a prize dope,
having reached already the end of my rope.
With blind eyes, where can I further grope?
Happening to meet Death by chance,
I kiss goodbye to Life's romance,
and tear up my Invitation to the Dance.

TWO SOUND-ALIKE WORDS, FRAMED BY TIME
(SEMI-DIALOGUE)

Everybody got born, to help fill the world with new, helpless people whom the birth-givers are obliged to take care of and be responsible for, whether they do so or not.

Much later, death of those same new people affords exchange room on earth for the on-parading, even newer generation.

Well, that's a nice historical succession.

Yes, it's called "take your turn," or "your turn next." You're only a humble part of it, but you count.

In the long run, the death numbers precisely equal the old birth numbers, when math reckoning takes effect.

They go on mounting, but keep pace with each other, like numerical twins in time's so-far endless process.

The words "process" and "progression" are sound-alikes.

GOING OPPOSITE THE WELCOME MAT,
UNDIGNIFIED, TO BE SPIT AT.
DISHONORED INTO THE GRAVE,
WHETHER WE WERE COWARDLY OR BRAVE.

When life fades to its declining years,
we're bundled up and put away
in nursing homes to be cared for
like babies helpless recently born.
We're torn away from independence
and organized into units.
We're guided like sheep or infants.
Old age. We're hopelessly led to die
with rebelling memories that wish to stay
in independent self-sufficient array.
But memories are impotent to reclaim that day.
So we sink down into our hellhole graves,
dim of our former consciousness.
We're treated like inanimate objects,
totally powerless to object.
We take up ultra-valuable space,
and placed in the category of "erase,"
without the benefit of dignity or grace.

A SO-CALLED FUTURE

Throughout my life, I've always had some kind of future.
But now, at ninety plus, I barely have any.
So I proceed to invent imaginary ones
that serve as unreachable daydreams
describing a whole lot of impractical schemes.
All the stationery I waste in reams
to write down these elaborate devices

can be crumbled up. And my future's gone,
like a dead old swan on a dirty pond
I spend remaining life to ponder upon.
Why not my own human past,
whose effect on me was so vast?
I too much mourn that it couldn't last.
Before that, it was one big beautiful blast.
My bony hand crumbles my baldness
into bundles of imaginary hair
that realistically just aren't there.
My brainless skull conceives of cloudless air
in an empty universe where corpses stare.
Am I then about to croak?
I'm sorry. This is no joke.
So now that I'm about to relinquish my state,
with whom can I conduct an endless debate?
Myself, if I can find him,
so continually assigned him.
Together, we'll be both dim.

REMEMBERING JIMMY STAGNO.
HERE I AM, BUT HE HAD TO GO.

Loving friendship, now permanently perished,
frustrates me. I so cherished
his dear personal contact,
I wish we had drawn up a contract
that whoever survives, with the other dead,
keeps reloading the nostalgia in my head,
in painful reminder of what I lost.
Daily and nightly, I keep paying the same cost,
making death the outstanding unpunished crime.
This is so bitter and sweet at the same time

that it's a one-way street in this snarled traffic rhyme.
Well, I'm helpless to renew
the exquisite friendship that was literally true.
Till stopped, it amazed us how it continually grew.

BEING YOUNG AND BEING OLD
ARE REVERSE SIDES OF THE SAME FOLD.
IN NEITHER EXTREME COULD I BE BOLD.
MY WELL-BEING HAS ALREADY BEEN SOLD.

Is lust the physical side of love?
Is love the spiritual side of lust?
Is oxidation the decayed side of rust?
Is enticement a side of ass and bust?
How can I tell? I'm not a chemist.
Science is all very well.
But what are the laws of the universe?
Fill loads of money in the purse
via the medium of bank account,
and then watch your finance mount.
Do your math and count.
Once you get to the right sum,
you're beyond infancy, when you sucked your thumb
and called incessantly for your Mum.
How you bawled when she wouldn't come!
But then when I achieved maturity,
I stopped being needy, due to older security.
Thus I grew up, but too much.
Mom isn't available to my infantile touch,
and old age is scary. I fear death
and such symptoms of failing breath.
Thus, I'm in a bind.
What next will I find?

Please don't tell me right now.
I can't take it, despite being a highbrow.

THE UPSHOT
OF YOUR DOWNSHOT.
WAS IT A PERNICIOUS PLOT?

When miserable melancholy and depression
lower your mood, you need a session
with a new merry-maker,
who'll be a shaker
of your general disposition
into such a new good mood
that never ever again will you brood.
Let him be such a comic
as to be a remedial tonic.
You'll laugh so hard, your stomach will split,
making you fall down deep Death's pit.
In that pit you inspire pity,
so you'll forget that clown's being so awfully witty.

TO A HEAVEN SEEKER
WHOSE REMOTE POSSIBILITY CAN'T BE BLEAKER

Being dead is impossible to recover from,
so the very attempt identifies you as dumb.
Give up your determination for life's renewal.
What organic matter can you use as fuel?
Whoever ridicules you, challenge him to a duel,
with the loser having the right to be called a fool.
Idiotic stupidity rules the underworld,
where the acute brains of intellect are never unfurled.

Being dead is an inescapable trap,
in the form of a package you can never unwrap,
whose ribbons are permanently knotted,
which is the way Death originally had it plotted.
Therefore heaven is out of your reach,
like feeding a dead whale on a sandy beach.

A PONY ONLY

I spent my life building up today's nostalgia
for youth's sweet time that I'll never re-live
except for phony memories that time will give.
Why is memory so phony?
It's like as a boy I was given a pony
to ride on, instead of a real genuine horse
which my parents wouldn't give,
but I begged them till I was hoarse.
For those early days, I now have remorse.
For my dearest wish, my parents wouldn't endorse.
They were the villains, I was the victim.
They were too strict with me.
They're dead now, so that was their fee
that I belatedly imposed.
Like a sweet innocent victim I posed.
They're rotting in hell now, I supposed.
I got my revenge on my parents.
It was obviously transparent.

SUGARCOATING DEATH
WITH A SWEETENING ELIXIR
FOR A ROMANTIC FIXTURE

You sink into the amorous arms of Death,
who kisses away your final breath,
and conveys you to eternity's honeymoon.
How orderly for you to swoon!
Death loves your easy submission
to his otherwise morbid commission.
In this romantic atmosphere,
don't spoil it by introducing the note of fear.
You and divine Death must call each other "dear."
You're his eternally sexy bride,
so agree sweetly to his taking you for a ride.
Death is such a seductive sweetheart
that he's only doing, per script, his part.
Now it's time for you to faint away
and allow night to steal your previous day.

THE "MEMORY WITHIN TIME" DIALOGUE

Is life one thing after another?

Yes, but sometimes mentally we reverse that order.

How do you mean?

Reminiscences aren't always chronological.

What's your point?

Sometimes we think of child memories after delving into recent
ones.

Sure. Memories tumble all over each other in mangled and jumbled
temporal disorder.

They're a miscellaneous bunch of haphazardousnesses.

Our brains keep an awfully sloppy record, from the point of view of when the occurrences actually did occur.

You mean *when* it was, that they took chronological place?

Yes, from time's retroactive perspective.

As a person, you're very reflective.

Yes, in the context of being retrospective.

Are you keeping your memory in good shape?

Some slip away, but then others take their place.

There are so many to go around.

Some are trivial, but others profound.

Some are lost, but then may be swiftly found.

After long elapse, they then can be rediscovered on the ground.

Keep being the vigilant detective hound.

Death simultaneously erases them all.

That's when uniformly they all at once fall,
since your brain is gone, which stored them all.

That's when Death may well be accused of gall
for interfering with our personal records.

Yes. Death sure can do prolific wrecking,
but you can't summon him in hasty becking.

I WAS SPARED FROM THE SECOND WORLD WAR, BEING TOO YOUNG TO SACRIFICE MY GORE. NOW I'M OLD, SO I HAVE LESS IN STORE.

With Death are you being preoccupied?
If I say "no," I will have lied.
Death is consuming me night and day
in the mental arena of my mind.
Physically, I'm also being left behind.
Between them both, it's an impossible grind.
Death is attacking from two sides,
like America dealt with both Germany and Japan
during the famous Second World War.
History is measured by what went before.
So many people had to spend their gore,
whereas mine is thinning out,
which is why I'm much less stout.
I forgot what war is all about.

A DIAGNOSIS OF DEATH BY A NON-DOCTOR

Death is a chronic disease
that will never cease?
No, it's a disciplined lack
that will never come back.
It's memory's loss
of whatever took place,
so what actually happened
is denied and negated,
permanently belated.
Once Death is encountered
as a non-event
that can never arise

to meet the next sunrise,
it's abandoned surprise.
Whatever's there, you don't get,
unaccompanied by regret.
This total lack of emotion
won't admit your old pal's devotion,
so there's no mourning
to greet the next morning.

UNRESOLVED PUZZLE

Life includes so many things, that I don't know what to make of it.
Its complexity bewilders me.

Why not just live it?

But that does't solve its mystery.

Just live out its mystery. Ride it.

But will it penetrate my knowledge?

Leave it to its own device.

But I want to understand what life is all about.

Isn't it just instinctive and intuitive?

Now you're resorting to mysticism.

But can't I just invent reality?

It doesn't work that way. Reality just *is*.

Plain and simple?

Don't make more of it than what it is.

But I'm impatient.

Why bother? Just relax.

But you have to relax *from* something.

Then just exert yourself.

No, that's too arbitrary.

Are you trying to create meaning?

It just turns out that way.

Well, build on it.

What is "it"?

You're too reductive.

THE QUANDARY OF LIFE
INCLUDING DOUBTS AND INSECURITY

Being alive is full of complications,
especially being scared of death.
It's a trial to make ourselves comfortable.
We face power struggles, and rivalry.
It's serious business, where humor is inserted,
as a form of comic relief.
Other people in our lives help or hinder.
Growing up can be painful and unfair.
Jealousy and envy make comparisons.
Why are others often better off?
How can we all get along?
Let's give ourselves pleasure that's legal.
We have to watch our step, along the way
and get what we need, get what we want.
No wonder we need help.
It's all so precarious, sometimes.
Can we have too much? Too little?
What's fair?
We shouldn't be greedy.
We're going too far.

They'll punish you. Watch out.
You're being under watch, evaluated.
Can you hold your own, and not be an underdog?
Where do you fit in?
Who should you cling to?
Can you form a group?
Give me more power.
I could come to harm.
Protect me.

IS "THEN" WITHIN "NOW"?
SURE. AND HOW!

Thinking back into the past
puts me in another world
that I'm virtually a stranger to.
What are my dead friends doing there?
Images pop up and disappear.
It's far away, but almost near.
It's me that used to be,
traveling in inner space.
I'm here, but they're only there.
Do we cross tracks?
Are there trains in the picture?
Or cars, and I'm driven?
They drive, but I don't know how.
That's the way things are now,
as things shuffle around.
Am I on solid ground?
Thus I hold myself aloof
from what's floating in the air.
I take it in, and stare.
I'm a near-sighted me

balancing inner vision and what I see.
Soon the world will come into focus
and the instruments all align.
This is near the end of the line.
My organs are still intact.
But what's their impact?

MY NON-BELIEF
CAUSES GRIEF
FOR MY LOCAL PRIEST.

Since it's obvious common sense
that heaven does not exist,
how foolish to persist!
You'll never get your wish.
But you keep trying if you're dense,
without having a reasonable defense.
You die into a skeleton and skull,
and your passionate religion turns dull.
Death defeats religion all the time,
and makes praying a silly crime.
Now you've become an empty ghost.
Atheism welcomes you as your host.
But your mind is all shot to pieces,
having wasted life on following Jesus.
But if your stupidity was still liable,
you died being stuck inside the Bible.

ACHIEVING A MASSIVE GROWTH

What I used to do in youth,
old age now denies me that truth,
so my capacity is too low
to be in that vital flow.
I don't have the hormones
to drive my lady to moans.
Nowadays, she's reduced to groans.
My cock isn't hard enough
to fill her completely up.
I don't blast away at her cup.
So she has to use her own fingers
to trick herself into what lingers.
Old age drives me to shame
that my body is much too lame
to maneuver it and aim.
Does my lady forgive me?
Not when she'll outlive me.
She'll look at my impotent corpse
long minus its vanished force,
that had the semen of a young horse.
I used it to give birth to a colt.
From its mare it leapt out with a bolt,
and soon achieved a massive growth.

DELAYING DEATH
TILL HE ALMOST RUNS OUT OF BREATH

I'm too old to have a future,
so I'll look back instead,
now that I'm nearly dead.
I review all the scenes of youth

and revel in their accurate truth.
I romped with so many now-dead friends
who met relatively unfortunate ends
by precociously being death's victims
by having something wrong with their systems.
If health can sustain your life,
it's worth putting up with extra strife.
Seek longevity
when opposed to brevity.
Don't hurry up to fill that cavity
with the miserable corpse of your former body.
Better to remain, however crazy and dotty.
If you make death terribly impatient,
flatter him as his future patient.
Beg him to visit you soon,
for instance tomorrow afternoon,
as the chosen date for your assigned ruin.
Then he'll leap upon you with a pounce,
and devour you every ounce.

**KEEP GOING, UNTIL
YOU'VE RUN OUT OF DETERMINED WILL
TO BLOCK DEATH'S USUAL KILL.**

Make sure you remain alive,
with the ultimate aim to survive.
"Safety First" should be your motto.
Then everything else will follow,
with a coward's extreme caution
being your characteristic portion
of your personality attributes.
Such tendency will bear fruits
in lifelong maintaining,

which feeds your ever productive gaining
to objectively achieve your goal,
which is: to the end remain whole
till finally you fall apart:
a masterpiece of Death's art.
There's nothing left of you at all
except total negation with your fall
that uprises the utmost appall.
Back to your mother's womb you crawl.
Now your voyage is complete,
and with other corpses you compete.
Any compromises you delete.
You've become an embryonic worm
with the inability to squirm.

HOW YOU STOPPED BEING

When time runs out,
it's death-time, no doubt.
The transition was made,
and you're unmade.
It was a trade.
So now, as a rookie corpse,
you're a new spent force.
Your passivity is helpless
for any revival.
Death is no longer your rival.
It's clearly won the bout,
so hear the umpire's shout:
"Three strikes and you're out!"
You creep to the clubhouse,
followed by a chorus of boo's
not designed to give you a boost.

If you were bread, you're now toast,
which is not any food to boast.
You're ashore on your last coast.
Emptiness is your new host.
Its generosity is not the most,
but easily the least.
Death was your killer beast
who consumed you in an ornate feast.
Afterward he continually belched,
and had to loosen his belt.
You were part of his dung,
from his ass-cleft so breezily sprung.

"THE FITTEST SURVIVE."
DIALOGUE BY TWO OLD MEN

We're both getting so old simultaneously, that by the next time we meet, it might not happen.

Why not?

One of us might be dead.

Who? Which one?

Either. Or both. Does it matter?

It *vitally* matters to *me*.

The same with me.

Is this competitive?

Sure. That's what life is, according to evolution's theory, called "The Fittest Survive."

But the theory doesn't apply here. This is America. The theory's inventor, Darwin, was English.

But aren't men and women evolutionarily the same anyway?

No. They're divided into genders.

Isn't that in Darwin's book?

Yes, but he was generalizing, in condescension to Americans.

The snob! I refuse to read his book.

Don't bother. Most of our states have banned it anyway.

What's the difference between politics and anatomy?

Read the book, if you ever find a liberal enough bookstore in these United States.

THE MODEST OLD MAN

I'm so old that I'm soon about to die. But I hate to leave this old life without first becoming famous. Any suggestions?

Were you an artist or a writer who could quickly summon your paintings or books into a celebrity exposure, guaranteeing you public fame?

No. I was never creative.

Then you'll have to die without having achieved fame.

But could I fake it?

How? Never having been creative? I'm at a loss as to what to advise.

I'll have to give up and die unfamous.

That's very modest of you.

I feel comfortable in a low key. Why make a phony splash? I'll be dying with good authentic character, despite having nothing to show for it.

Won't your corpse do?

No, it's too commonplace and plebeian.

Then you'll have to settle for modesty as your most becoming attribute.

It's not becoming—I already achieved it. Give me credit.

TRANSITION BETWEEN POLARITIES

(1)
The time slot
to go from "be" to "not."
The immediately before
and immediately after,
are not a matter of laughter.
But your mourning survivors,
after they bury,
may now make merry.
They have a wake
from which you don't awake.

(2)
When getting old gets out of hand,
arriving at the danger state
of death's becoming a reality
to actually kill you,
then you're compelled to take notice
and helplessly "deal" with it
before the "too late" bell rings.
Then the emergency is in the past,
and death strangles you, aghast.
That was your last fling.
How strange that you're in the "past tense,"
and stay in this new time slot forever.
Your doom has already taken place.
So consciousness is cut off

like water from a faucet.
Too late now to force it.
To call a plumber is laughable.
So tragedy turns to comedy,
and the curtain falls on your play,
with the audience filing out.
You're done: no doubt.
The audience got entertained.
Their collective consciousness still reigned.
You were only the subject matter,
which for "you" now doesn't matter,
being no longer composed of matter.
A corpse doesn't count.
It's a no-account.

MY THEME IS LIFE'S END, HAVING JUST TURNED THE CORNER AND GONE ROUND THE BEND.

For continued life, prevent death
from interfering with your breath
and causing your lungs to malfunction,
like weeping while peeling an onion.
Death's job is to murder you
with malice and destructive energy,
which designates death as your enemy.
Without life, what can you ever be?
Only the subject of your previous history.
Your geography is limited to the grave,
where your prospects for survival are severely grave.
You have to spend eternity there,
and you can't even come out for air.
Your social life is thinly bare,

at the limit of your popularity.
Do I express myself with clarity?
I'll donate this essay to charity,
priced low enough for the meager purse
to afford, but with a growling curse.
At least they're warned that it could be worse.
I could have written this only in prose,
where the words could be washed out with a hose.

MORTALITY IS A DRAG.
THUS I'M ABOUT TO SAG.

Are you angry at yourself for passively allowing so much lifetime to accumulate as to now find yourself so helplessly an old man?

Where did it all go? I was once vibrating with dispensable youth, and now my body is a prisoner to becoming obsolete without my being able to do anything about it. I'm its victim, as time's prisoner.

Yes, it all happened to you. You're in a position of being unfairly old. It's not your fault.

The horrible sudden thing about this predicament is that I'm actually in danger of death.

While you weren't looking, old age crept up behind you and is now endangering your life—your very life, whose youth and middle age were taken advantage of as natural and inevitable.

What happened to me?

Too much of the progression of everything. You fell into the natural trap of finding yourself in this helpless predicament.

It's not comfortable. I may stop being, entirely.

That's so incomprehensibly serious.

Do you pity me?

How can I not? I'm prone to it too.

Your sympathy does nothing for me.

WE HAVEN'T HEARD YET

Despite various religious and cult superstitions, no one in human history has ever had an afterlife, like in heaven. He or she becomes a corpse, followed by gradually shrinking and hardening into a skeleton below and a skull above, unless cremated. Meanwhile, no former organs operate any more.

Living people would love to hear a first-hand report about afterlife conditions, including locations. But history hasn't recorded any such reports, which would sell out newspapers, not to mention break television records.

Sane scientists take this as lack of acceptable proof that there's ever been any viable information of post-life activities whatever, not even for saviors with or without followings.

This is news that would give heart and confirmation to atheists. But atheists don't want to antagonize religious believers, who may seek revenge of some sort. So superstition remains alive and kicking. But not, however, anyone who ever died.

HOW DEATH SNATCHED ME
AND DREADFULLY MATCHED ME,
TILL I BECAME COMPARATIVELY WEE,
WHEN I RAN BUT COULDN'T FLEE.

I loved life with all my heart,
but then I lost it
once I barely crossed it
to death's nearby territory.
It was a terror story.

Death grabbed me by the balls,
and my agony reverberated down the halls.
Now I'm put out of my misery
and become an item of small history
that makes me virtually hysterical.
But death is the one that's really empirical.
It lavished itself all over me,
and I ran right away, but I couldn't flee.
I made no progress in my strides,
while death resists and resides.
Plus, I was too dead, besides.
You heard me through these confides?
Please sympathize,
to cut my story down to size
in considering my demise,
which came at no actual surprise.

AS THE YEARS PASS BY,
YOUR YOUNGER MOURNERS PREPARE TO CRY.

Every day is a new day,
but old age is divided into years,
with their accompanying fears
of accumulation too heavy.
Then are you already ready?
The years that added up too vastly
have been wasted too rashly
accumulating their tottering pile,
making for death so worthwhile
to decimate the whole ordeal
(or rather is it a raw deal?)
under the ravages of a tank-like wheel.
Thus I'm being smothered,

who once at birth was mothered.
Old age is just next door
to shutting down life under death's bore.
So now you know the whole total score
registered on your smashed body.
Time was what you embody.

MOMENTARILY, I SEE THEM AGAIN.

I remember all my friends, but they're gone,
since my longevity buried them all.
Where? Naturally in death's thrall.
I have nostalgia for my old friends,
but also neuralgia when I get the bends.
I ask them where they have gone;
we used to have such fun together.
They look at me grimly, from death.
"Come over. Join us," they request.
But they're only acting polite,
issuing such a mock invitation,
that they're just pretending we'll all be on vacation
and have such fun together,
that not even a rainy day could spoil our pleasure,
that only comes with middle class leisure.
Goodbye, my friends. I weep for you.
Is it real about where I'm going? Is it true?

BEING CLOSE TO DEATH,
HERE'S WHAT I SAY WITH MY DYING BREATH.

Keeping alive
is my main drive.
The rest I put aside,
since my priority is my old age
that puts me in a cage
where death has me so trapped
that in my pants I almost crapped.
On my head, Death politely tapped,
and scared me by saying "You're next!"
He was only kidding, with that text,
designed to scare me.
My heart can't take it any more.
It will give me appleplexy.
With all my agony, women still seem sexy.
Well, that just about rubs it in.
I'm too old to ever win.
Death is my ruler, high above.
What I miss most about my failing life is love.
Yet I have it! My wife still lives.
She's there to weep when death gives.
But what if she goes first?
We're matched, but we can't rehearse.
It's too late to do the research.
Things look gloomy, from my perch.

HOW LIFE KEEPS GOING FOR THE MASS,
BUT WE OLDIES GET KICKED OUT ON OUR ASS.
THAT'S HOW OUR GENERATIONS WILL PASS.

Life is the best thing we have, so let's keep it up as long as possible.

But meanwhile, time is passing, so youth is fled, middle age passed through, and old age debilitating us, and death intimately lurking.

It sounds like brevity,
but it's actually longevity.

Old age is wise.
But it faces demise.

I'll be gone forever?

But the world is replenished by new babies all the time, thanks to split-gendered sex, the product of evolution.

It takes two to tangle.
That's reproduction's angle.

To make room for babies, we old folks have to die.

But we stick it out as long as possible.

We so hog the earth,
to make room for new birth.

How noble that we oldies sacrifice personal lives to keep the world going.

Where is it flowing?

Out of our sight.
What an awful blight!

Thus death snatches us all,
and in plentiful heaps we fall.
History records it all
to console our mutual fall.

YOUNG MOURNS OLD AT MEMORIAL, GIVING A TUTORIAL PRESIDED ON BY CUSTODIAL. THEY TALK OF THE FAMILY PLOT, WHICH IS A BEAUTIFULLY KEPT LOT.

The young in each other's arms
mean kisses more than harms,
and emphasize their own charms.
Then they breed children
who attend their funerals
and give memorial speeches
for those dead members of the species.
Their grandchildren, by generation,
give a belated oration,
watching films for remembrance
of the old family members.
Death replaces life quick,
which is time's nasty trick.
Where's the new architecture, brick for brick?
In history, nothing will lengthily stick
except the same old human stuff
that ripely repeats without a bluff.
Humanity's familiar passions
survive the passing fashions.
Old genes make new people
bound to fade when feeble,
subjected to mourners' weeping
out of tradition's keeping.
To call the dead euphemistically "sleeping"
is the term to soften the blow
of the venerable member gone below
with his memories to bestow.

THE POOR OLD MAN (WHO REALLY LOOKS THE PART, OUT IN THE OPEN, UNHIDDEN)

I'm an old man, not only in the amount of accumulated years (early nineties), but also *looking* the role, as if I were type-cast for the movies.

Well, that's honest of you not to deceive other people, in being what you actually are.

That's proven in the way people react to me, as if I'm in need of their help just to move around.

Do they act like they pity you?

Not only that, but they act afraid of being contaminated by my unfortunate condition.

They avoid you?

I'm ashamed to admit that.

Well, I don't blame them. They're only being honest in wanting to protect themselves from the polite threat of being your undesirable companion.

They want nothing to do with me. I'm no fun for anyone. I would hold them back, hold them down.

On that note, I must go now, having an appointment elsewhere.

Is it urgent?

Of course.

I'm appalled by your selfish honesty, that verges on deception. Nice knowing you. Good luck for the rest of your so-called life, if you call it that. *(Leaves.)*

(Now alone.) Well, that illustrates an example of what I've come to. I'm pitiably alone. Death is throwing hints at me.

(DEATH enters.) (DEATH:) I sure am. Come on.

TWO OLD MEN ABOUT TO DIE
ARE ENOUGH EVEN TO MAKE
THE UNSENTIMENTAL CRY.
(MORBID DIALOGUE)

Your life security is endangered by having grown extremely old, at
an unstoppable rate.

I'm helpless to slow it down.

Death would then be your next stop. As your old friend, I'll say
goodbye now. Later might be too late.

But you're old enough yourself to precede me.

Then let our goodbyes be not only mutual, but simultaneous.

Preparing for our dismal futures is a melancholy endeavor.

Our friendship is behind us, receding into the bleak past.

In the old days, we were so carefree.

Let's somehow magically renew them.

No, just review them, but my memory is worn out
and crumpled up, no longer stout.

Doom is nigh. What else are we about?

At least we have a priority,
so we're not lost entirely.

It's still a hard act to follow,
with our insides so hollow.

Is that because we haven't eaten?

No. Just simply because we're beaten,
to the point that there's no more cake to sweeten.

So if we have no more teeth to rot,
then we have to thank death a lot.

Death will exult, taking us both,

thus doubling its solemn oath.

Is its maw wide enough?

It can accommodate lots of stuff,
an opportunity unlikely to muff.

So taking the two of us at once
is expedient, even for a dunce.

HOW TO EXTEND YOUR LIFE,
EVEN AT THE EXPENSE OF EXTRA STRIFE

Be careful not to die too soon.
You see the heart specialist this afternoon.
Tomorrow you see the dermatologist.
Next week you see the urologist.
Health insurance has got you covered
for only a nominal fee, you discovered.
How lucky that you're working the system
with such a load of practical wisdom!
Preserving your life is a deed so automatic
that philosophically you're resorting to the pragmatic.
With Government assistance, you don't live in the attic.
If any ailment plagues you, attack it.
Then your life is spared for more years
as long as your payments are not in arrears.
A happy scream will dance between your ears.
Your chest is shouting to lose all its fears.
Reassurance is the key to equilibrium.
So from your voice is lilting a joyful hum.
It's like being protected by your dear old mom,
who took care of you from the start
with her fine maternal art.

ARE YOU O.K. AFTER WAKING UP?

When "life" resumes after sleep, you were right not to feel any danger in interrupting your wakeful stream of consciousness for the sake of sleep's peaceful rest and bodily restoration back into resumed energy.

I didn't feel like a courageous hero facing and overcoming danger, when I allowed myself to "nod off." So don't give me unnecessary credit for heroism.

It's very peacefully reassuring to feel confident that you'll safely and automatically wake up again after your routine "adventure" into the innocent non-adventure of sleep, that incurred no risk.

Good. Thank you. I'm too modest and unassuming to hog unmerited credit.

I value your honesty and no-nonsense approach.

Still, its fun to realize that it's safe not to bother to fear that I won't wake up again, and that my life is not over when I do awake. It was an imaginary safe fear that gave me a spurious kick or frisson—a naughty thrill—like a dangerous adventure over a waterfall in a flimsy canoe. It's like a child teasing herself at a scare movie of terror and horror. An imaginative plunge.

How fanciful you are!

NOT DEFINING LIFE

Can you define life?

No. It's too vague and mysterious.

Is it amorphous?

That's the explanation I would use, to get out of being asked to define it.

Is it a weak excuse? A cop-out?

No. Life is too ambiguous to presumptuously define.

If defining it would be presumptuous, then that's your excuse not to attempt it.

How many excuses do I need?

As many as justifying your refusal to try defining it.

Then you won't ask any more?

That's co-operative with your evasive wishes.

CHALLENGING A TEST, WITH A DEFENSIVE ACCUSATION

How are you?

Oh what a banal question, socially automatically superficial!

But I really mean it, out of genuine concern.

Why? What happened?

You were ill.

Maybe I forgot.

Do you have dementia?

I hope not.

What's today's date?

The day after yesterday, and the one before tomorrow.

You're evading my test.

Am I cheating?

Yes, to cover up your memory loss.

Do I have one?

Apparently.

You're so vague.

Is that a complaint? You're not fair.

LIFE IS ONE TO A CUSTOMER

What does life mean to you?

Everything. That's what I am.

You are life?

No, not in general. In particular.

You're just one of many?

That's all I'm limited to, or even entitled to. I'm an example.

You can't be a greedy hog, like an exploitative capitalist? You just have to accept what you're given.

Only me.

Isn't that enough?

It ought to be. Unless I'm a movie star, and play roles.

IRRITABILITY DIALOGUE

Does life ever get too much for you?

Yes. Then I try to calm down, take a deep breath or two, and get back my nerves.

Do you succeed?

Most of the time.

Then you're lucky, unlike me. If life gets too much for *me*, I become neurotic and blow my top, in a confused frenzy.

Poor you. I feel sorry for you. I would have lost my head.

If you had lost your head, your both shoulders might have collapsed in the middle and damaged your central chest clavicle.

Your scenario is grotesque, and maybe even inaccurate.

Sorry. I went too far. Anatomical architecture has been with us for centuries, and shouldn't be molested.

I should hope not. I was about to lose my temper, thanks to your insinuating I was inaccurate.

How touchy you are! Do I have to handle you with kid gloves?

Don't you dare!

That's too imperative to disobey.

COMPARING TWO BIG LIES

I'm afraid and horrified of death. It's so permanent!

It's a hard nut to swallow. But if you're willing to delude yourself, then believe in heaven and eternal life, as Christ advocated.

He indicated that heaven and eternal life came through him himself.

What arrogance!

But he won multiple followers every generation since, though slightly dying out by now.

Well, they formed a confraternity.

That's no excuse. Vast numbers of human believers don't add up to truth and veracity. Illusion is illusion, even by the mass.

But isn't it mercifully soothing of the fear and horror of permanent death, to believe in the mercy of heaven and eternal life, like Christ advocated, putting it all on himself?

No. It's poor cowardly delusionality, like believing, along with Trump, in having won a second presidential term, like a "big lie."

Christ's big lie dwarfs Trump's by far, and much more permanently. He won the greatest fame.

Poor Trump. He was outclassed.

Don't feel sorry for him. His followers were ferocious.

Some still are. But maybe it's calming down.

We'll see. He's still influential, like his predecessor.

DEATH'S DOUBLE LACK OF MERCY
(DIALOGUE BY TWIN OLDIES)

I'm ninety-one plus, so my life expectancy is getting reduced every minute.

At ninety-one plus, that's natural. Hold on as long as you can, but then let go.

I can't resort to magic.

Of course not. Accept your doom.

Your advice is clear cut.

Go off peacefully.

No. With protest.

Suit yourself. Your natural reluctance can't help you to ward off death.

My body is failing.

How inevitable! But I'm in the same boat.

How?

You're my twin.

Then I excommunicate you as a brother.

Don't bother. That's death's business.

It interferes with our family life.

Whoever goes first will be pre-jealous of the other's momentary survival delay.

Envious, not jealous.

We'll split the difference.

CLEANING UP DEATH'S STINK, PREFERABLY AT THE SINK

Don't sniff death too close,
or it may contaminate your clothes.
If a corpse is a genuine stiff,
smell it to get a whiff.
Death is a horrible event.
Does it protrude indecent scent?
No, just the scent of fear and dread
that the sweating victim had shed.
Then the poor corpse has to be cleaned up,
with chloroform perhaps.
For the funeral ceremony,
cleanliness must carry decorum
in civilized solemnity.
Then for the memorial, be neatly clad.
Your fellow near-by guests will be glad.
Don't be afraid of foul odor.
Perhaps it's cleaned up in soda,
provided you remain sober.
Thus the sense of smell is wiped clean
to sanitize death's terrible stink.
It requires bubbly soap at the sink.
Laundrify all foul remnants.
Hygiene is recruited to civilize death.

Funeral guests emit alcoholic breath
to powerfully overcome foul vestiges of death.
Be hygienic at graveyard cemetery
to purify enemy traces:
the sanctified odor of graces.

THE FUTILITY HUNTER

The older in my old age I get, the more carefully and methodically I plan for the future. Yet, while death looms ever closer, those very plans get more endangered to become abandoned or cut short.

That's an ironically bad break; having your carefully prioritized plans in proximate danger of discontinuation the more you age with venerably vulnerable frailty! Incidentally, how old *are* you?

Ninety-one plus.

Wow! Go ahead and consider your plans decidedly endangered, in their prioritized commitments.

Poor me!

You eligible death candidate! Your hat's really in the ring.

What's that a metaphor for?

Futility.

(Determined:) Not if I can help it!

But your longevity proceeds gradually to weaken you.

Not if I can help it.

You dogged snarler! You're heading into disappointed frustration directly, with eyes stupidly open.

Isn't failure life's essence?

What a goal!

HOW YOUR MOURNERS RESPOND
TO SHOW THAT THEY WERE FOND

Life is only one to a customer,
making you specifically unique,
with your own brain and physique.
But then you decline from your peak.
Decay has made you weak.
You crumble up and die,
being cut off from life's supply,
which is too fatal to revive from.
No wonder your mourners look glum.
At the funeral parlor, they spit out their gum.

I DIED IN NEW YORK CITY,
LEAVING MY WIFE, WHO WAS SO PRETTY
THAT I DIDN'T MIND PLAYING WITH HER TITTY.
(SORRY TO BE SO BAWDY.
IT'S NOT OFTEN THAT I'M SO NAUGHTY.)

Life is terribly wonderful,
a neat and lovely bundle
that makes it hard to grumble.
Then who comes along? Death,
who by depriving you of breath
destroys your life line,
shoving you into decline,
till your wife could no longer call you "mine."
From her tears, her eyes took a shine
that reflected the brazen sun.
From all the slovenly corpses, you were one.
When your wife had to bury you,
she recalled how merry were you.

So she burst out with a laugh:
"He was too clever by half.
But he was indeed so witty
that he described the many ways I was pretty
while he was toying with my raised titty.
All this took place in New York City.
I slumped on his lap so curled,
it felt like the safest place in the world.
He smiled as only he could smile.
The photo dangles from my memory file."

AFTERWORD: REPRESSING THE PAST

(Marvin Cohen talking to Bill and Williams Cole.)

MC: Of what percentage of the past are you reluctant to go into because the memories are too sad or unbearable?

BC: Nothing.

MC: Nothing?

BC: No.

MC: I have things some people like myself included wiped out and repressed; some memories of the past because they were too uncomfortable.

BC: Were you snubbed? Made to stand on the other side of the playground?

MC: Whenever I was embarrassed or socially disgraced or excluded or made a mockery of, my self, my dignity, whenever I socially fell so far below that it would seem as if I could never be rectified—

WC: Do you have bad memories of those?

MC: I don't know they're all repressed! *(Laughs.)* And they're all in the lovely lovely never-never land of denial! *(Everyone laughs.)*

[*Transcript of video made by Williams Cole ©2000, youtu.be/ j4J8QQan4Lg*]

ABOUT THE AUTHOR

Marvin Cohen (born July 6, 1931), is the author of a number of episodic novels, plays and verse, a book on baseball, and several collections of shorter pieces—stories, dialogues, parables, and idiosyncratic essays. His work has also appeared in more than 100 publications, from the experimental to the mainstream, including: *Ambit, Antaeus, Assembling* ("a collection of otherwise unpublishable writings"), *The Beat Scene* (alongside Kerouac, Ginsberg, and Corso), *Chelsea, Fiction, The Hudson Review, Thomas Merton's Monks Pond, New Directions in Prose and Poetry, The Transatlantic Review, The New York Times, Harper's Bazaar* and *Vogue*.

Cohen was born in Brooklyn, New York City. He has described himself as one who has "risen from lower-class background to lower-class foreground." He studied art at Cooper Union but left college to focus on writing. He supported himself with a series of short-term jobs including mink farmer and merchant seaman. He later taught creative writing at various New York colleges. He is married and currently lives with his wife in Manhattan.

ACKNOWLEDGMENTS

The author and publisher would like to thank the following individuals for their generous financial support, which helped to make this publication of *Trying to Fool Death* a reality:

Jeziel Adams, Kevin Adams, Alfie, Micah Altman, Wax Banks,
Ross Barkan, Thomas Young Barmore Jr, Tara Barnes, Melissa Beck,
Sam Bertram, Brad Bigelow (The Neglected Books Page), Carl W Bishop,
Brian R. Boisvert, Michael H. Broder, Jennifer Brooker, David Brownless,
Wayne L. Budgen, Marco Buscaglia, Gabriele Caredda, Tobias Carroll,
Scott Chiddister, Adam Cipriani, Joel Coblentz, Sadie Cocteau,
Mike Cooper (U.K.), Costa, Nicholas Croft, Parker & Malcolm Curtis,
Joshua Doughty, Robert E, Andrew Eagle, Isaac Ehrlich, Cassey Eisch,
Myrhat Eliot, Dayna Epley-Kazor, Veronika Ferdman, Fred Filios,
Michael Flory, Thea Flurry, Deanna Leonie Gabb, Thomas Gagnon,
James Gallagher, Justin Gallant, Gordon Gearhart, Adam Gerhart,
GMarkC, B. F. Gordon, Jr., Baron Anthony Gualtieri, Everett Haagsma,
Stan Halstead, Heather Harkins, Beverly Jean Harris, Haya, Aric Herzog,
Dave Holets, J. Holmes, Ania Honess, Conor Hultman,
Peter and Deborah Jackson, Derek Jellison, Jevi, Neil Jacobson,
Fred W Johnson, Jacob H Joseph, Alex Juarez, Andrew Kahn,
Rebekah Kass, Jim Ramsey Khouri, Beth A. King, Jim Klumper,
Sergey Kochergan, Stefan Kruger, Paul Kuliev, C. S. Labairon,
Susie LaBarre, The Ladinsky Family, Jean-Jacques Larrea for Isidore
Pomerance, Chaz Larson, J. A. Lee, Gardner Linn, Joan Livingston,
Nick Long, cam lorendo, the one and only Larry Luddecke,
Nelson R. Lugo, Marcel, V. Markosian, Jim McElroy, Donald McGowan,
Michael McGrath, William Messing, Lee Millen, Ardell Miller,
Jason Miller, Miss Fats, J.L. Mock, Spencer F Montgomery, Steven Moore,
MJ Moriarty, Geoffrey Moses, Gregory Moses, Scott Murphy,
Anthony Notaro, Richard Novak, Michael O'Shaughnessy,
Sarah Olmstead, Trevor Owens, Andrew Pearson, Holly Marie Peterson,
K. Peterson, Rachel L Peterson, zasu pitts, Andrija Popovic, Quintin,
Armando Ramirez III, Judith Redding, Ryan C. Reeves,
Sheridan Delaine Youngblood Reid, Ken Rokos, Rebecca S, John Salis,
Florian Schiffmann, Seda, R Shinn, Yvonne Solomon, K. L. Stokes,
Kayla Stroup, Gustav Szlosek, Kate Torgerson,

triton7070@sbcglobal.net, Chad Michael Van Alstin, Eris Wadham, Barry Wallenstein, Christopher Wheeling, WHJJr, Karl Wieser, Charles Wilkins, T.R. Wolfe, WovenPixel (Danie Evans), Elaine Y., The Zemenides Family, and Anonymous